FOUR GUYS
in a BOAT

FOUR GUYS
in a BOAT

WHAT'S THAT ALL ABOUT?

KJELL CHRISTOPHERSEN
JOHN CARNAHAN
ED VAN NULAND
and
JOHN "SKIPPER" SAWYER
with
G. M. BURROW

Published by Roman Roads Press
Moscow, Idaho 83843
www.romanroadspress.com

Kjell Christopherson, John Carnahan, Ed Van Nuland, John Sawyer, and G. M. Burrow, *Four Guys in a Boat: What's That All About?*

Copyright © 2018 by Kjell Christopherson, John Carnahan, Ed Van Nuland, John Sawyer, and G. M. Burrow.

Cover and interior design by Valerie Anne Bost.
Cover painting, *Four Guys in a Boat*, by Tom Garfield.

Printed in the United States of America.

All rights reserved. No part of this publication may be reproduced, stored in a retrieval system, or transmitted in any form by any means, electronic, mechanical, photocopy, recording, or otherwise, without prior permission of the author, except as provided by USA copyright law.

For our wives—Judi, Brenda, Janet, and Jan.
You're the greatest soulmates ever.

K.C., J.C., E.V., J.S.

For Oma, who loves the water.

G.M.B.

A B O U T   T H E   A U T H O R S

KJELL CHRISTOPHERSEN, economist and king, grew up sailing the Norwegian fjords. He has survived more near-death experiences than the other sailors combined, and if he were to have his way, each voyage would get considerably closer to death than they already do. He is recently retired from Emsi, and is married to the lovely Judi, who should have warned Skipper to up the insurance.

JOHN CARNAHAN is the resident adolescent in charge of each voyage's most acrobatic feats. He once appeared in an episode of *My Three Sons*, but his real passion is for Logos School, where he is the director of activities and also coaches the high school track team. His job is to tell Kjell what Kjell really wants in life. John is married to the fabulous Brenda and probably still gets carded.

Ed Van Nuland fell in love with the sea as a landlocked third-generation copper miner. He is the crew's mental librarian and raconteur extraordinaire, quoting poetry and spouting Shakespeare with his radio celebrity voice. He's a fan of bad ice cream and tends to get toothpaste and hydrocortisone mixed up. He is married to the adventurous Janet.

John "Skipper" Sawyer is the one who started the whole tradition by purchasing a sailboat when he had no clue how to sail. He teaches driver's ed (among other things) and is a former Marine, so nothing scares him, not even John Carnahan's driving. He's in charge of getting everyone home alive despite Kjell's best efforts. He is married to the blonde and gentle Jan, with whom he first learned to weigh anchor and sail towards adventure.

G.M. Burrow hates putting her face in the water and has never stepped foot in a sailboat, but she loves stealing stories and living vicariously, so that's okay. She's been writing real and made-up adventures since she was seven. She loves the Alps, adrenaline, and taking her eight nieces and nephews on merry escapades where hopefully at least one kid believes they're going to die.

CONTENTS

PROLOGUE	Four Guys in a Pub	1
CHAPTER ONE	Anacortes	13
CHAPTER TWO	Let the Adventure Begin	35
CHAPTER THREE	A Day in the Life	37
CHAPTER FOUR	Friday Harbor	53
CHAPTER FIVE	Like Old Friends Shaking Hands	61
CHAPTER SIX	Victoria	63
CHAPTER SEVEN	We Are Free	83
CHAPTER EIGHT	Deer Harbor	87
CHAPTER NINE	Roche Harbor	101
CHAPTER TEN	It Was Good	123

To young men contemplating a voyage,

I would say: Go.

—JOSHUA SLOCUM,
SAILING ALONE AROUND THE WORLD

It's not just a keel and a hull and a deck and sails.

That's what a ship needs.

But what a ship *is* . . . is freedom.

—CAPTAIN JACK SPARROW,
PIRATES OF THE CARIBBEAN

PROLOGUE

Four Guys in a Pub

~~~~~~~

> If you want to build a ship, don't drum up people
> to collect wood and don't assign them tasks and
> work, but rather teach them to long for the endless
> immensity of the sea.
>
> —ANTOINE DE SAINT-EXUPERY

At first, nobody knows how to answer. They look at each other around the table, beers in hand, a coke for Skipper. Am I asking a dog to explain why he wags his tail? Or have I touched on a mere hobby? Maybe just a habit?

Plenty of men throughout history have answered my question through songs and poems because in their very bones resides the yearning for white sails swelling over blue water, and nothing less than poetry will do. "My soul is full of longing for the secret of the sea, And the heart of the great ocean sends a thrilling pulse through me." (Longfellow, you soulful dude.)

My question was this. Why would four grandpas, all north of sixty, spend four days on a boat in the San Juan islands every summer for fifteen years, when only one grew up sailing and he, given the opportunity, might cheerfully capsize the boat?

"Deep and abiding fellowship," Ed says at length.

"I don't know about that," Skipper jokes.

But John agrees. "For me, camaraderie. It's about the four of us being together. The trip is secondary; it's a vehicle for—if you can believe it—just being with these guys."

"Of course I like the guys," Skipper adds easily. "But I'd go without them. Sailing is the one thing that's different than anything else you do. You're outdoors, on the water, no schedule. You can really set aside everything except morality." He is, as I discover later, capable of heavy understatement. He comes closest to sailing for the sake of sailing. If there's a Henry Wadsworth Longfellow on board, it may very well be Skipper.

Kjell speaks last. "It's something I look forward to the entire year. Last summer was our fifteenth voyage. I'm old enough to wonder, Can I go sixteen? Can I go seventeen? Can I go eighteen? Stretching the limits, year after year. I'm trying to tally it up."

So far, the crew is in general agreement. Very harmonious. But when the server of the sleek and crowded gastropub comes to take our orders—or tries to—I get a much more accurate look at this curious crew.

The shortest and, at seventy-four, the oldest, Kjell Christophersen is the one who grew up on the water and though he might deny it, his sparkling eyes and pumping fists convince me, yes, he would probably look on a knockdown as simply another adventure. He blows with the wind, one minute ordering a salad, the next caving to French fries (the waitress patiently scribbling) while John Carnahan fusses over him like a big sister, insisting that he himself knows what Kjell really wants.

John is sixty-three and the decided youngster, though a mere two years behind Ed and Skipper. Trim, tanned, silvered-haired, and blue-eyed, he has an infectious washboard laugh: a perfect laugh jouncing over a jolly road. With Kjell, he makes special use of his habit of grabbing you by the arm whenever he agrees, disagrees, loves, or disapproves of what you're saying—which proves hilarious because if there's anything that prompts Kjell to wave his short arms even more, it is someone grabbing his arm.

"I want beer and cheese mac," Kjell declares for a main dish.

The waitress says, "With bacon, kielbasa, or both?"

"Kielbasa," John interjects.

Maybe the meat options are confusing; maybe it's simply because John stuck his oar in, but Kjell impulsively withdraws the order. "Take everything back! Shhh, be quiet" (waving at John). "I want the lamb and ale stew!"

"No, you don't," John says. "You hate that . . ."

And so it goes.

Ed Van Nuland, through hard discipline, is less inclined to speak, but when he does, Shakespeare flows. Old-fashioned phrases like "Might I interject" and "You look swell" spill as easily as do spontaneous recitations from *Moby Dick*, *Macbeth*, and "The Rime of the Ancient Mariner." His vocal fluctuation itself pitches like a boat on heavy seas. With his ruddy cheeks and wide eyes and jolly girth, he looks rather German and says he feels "very Bavarian" with his pretzel—his light dinner choice. His is a voice of decisive authority that cuts through the sibling-like squabbling of John and Kjell, whom he calls "the Lilliputians." While those two are still arguing about lamb and ale stew, Ed leans over to me and says in an undertone: "I tune them out; I can't tolerate it. Eat whatever you want!"

John Sawyer, addressed as "Skipper" more out of respect than the need to avoid confusion with John Carnahan, is quietest, folding his arms and holding very still and rarely speaking his mind except to drop some easygoing sarcasm or to answer questions, and even then the other gents usually answer for him. He has gray hair, a thin white beard, quiet blue eyes. His dry voice sounds like sandpaper on pine wood. He calls the others "the lads" and sips his Coke through a straw and eats only half his ham and cheese sandwich. His demeanor holds the calm of a steady, weather-beaten hull. He is mild through and through. I find it fascinating that on the boat, this man's word is law.

Ordinary land-locked occupations (or retirement) is the name of the game for each man here in this tiny college town of Moscow, Idaho. "We respect each other not so much for what we are," Skipper says, "but for what we were." And you couldn't ask for a more scrambled hodgepodge of backgrounds.

From getting lost in the North Sea off the coast of Norway as a young teenager, to nearly being kidnapped by terrorists in the Philippines, to getting trapped in the US Embassy during the August 4, 1983 coup d'état in Ouagadougou, Kjell has seen more near-death experiences than the others combined. He has only recently eased out of the life of a roving economist to semi-retire at Emsi, a local software company he founded in 2000. His childish antics at the table bely a bold appetite for taking risks (he is famous for having thrown a rock at a Nazi as a mere toddler), not to mention his imposing epithet (Ed and John routinely introduce him as the King of Norway, which strangers readily believe) and a fearsome intellect. He is fluent in five languages, accepting phone calls on the side wherein he breaks into his native song-like Norwegian.

John is an old friend with the water, having grown up pummeled by the waves of Southern California and once spending four months on a university cruise ship which sailed from Los Angeles to Japan and Australia and back again. His claim to fame is that at ten years old, he appeared in an episode of *My Three Sons* and met Fred McMurray on set. His passion is for Logos School, where he is the director of activities and also a coach of the high school track team. He vows he is no daredevil ("I respect the water") even while admitting his addiction to reading plane-crash-in-water stories such as *Sully* or *The Perfect Storm*, especially while flying. "I want to go down!" His eyes light with adrenaline. (Kjell declares through a mouthful of French fries: "I am never going to fly with you.")

A third-generation copper miner, Ed (affectionately "Eddie" to John) was born in Butte, Montana, miles from the water. He holds a history degree and is the mental librarian of the crew; the brainpower in charge of hording details that the others forget. "He has the keenest memory of odd stuff I have ever known," Kjell says. After eighteen years in retail and nineteen years as the development director at Logos School, Ed spent some time as a local radio celebrity. With his announcer's elocution, I can see why.

Skipper is a former Marine—"Yet another reason why he is fearless and wonderful," Ed says, which sounds dramatic, but Skipper himself says his background was quite bland and he joined the Corps only due to lack of funds for college. Raised in an ultra conservative family who "never did anything bad—and believe me, the road was so narrow, you could have done something bad very easily," Skipper did his time in the Marines as an avionics mechanic, then earned his degree at the University of Idaho. He now teachers driver's ed and is the director of student services at New Saint Andrews College.

There might be nothing flashy about Skip, but he is the reason these four patchwork friends are drinking beer (and Coke) together around this bar-height table in the middle of a restaurant. It was Skip who, years ago, spontaneously bought a seventeen-foot sailboat for the exact amount he had in his savings, asked a friend to teach him to sail, and eventually took the classes necessary to charter larger boats in the San Juan Islands. In 2001, he invited the other three to join him.

Kjell boasts more glamorous seamanship, including vicarious experience through his relatives—gold-winning Olympic racers—and has himself raced against the then crown prince (now king) of Norway. But this is at least part of the reason he defers to Skipper. With

Skip's methodical discretion at the helm, Kjell can urge whatever risks he wants; Skipper is there to anchor them within their limits and get everyone home alive.

"I probably had more experience than these guys in the beginning," Kjell says modestly, "but they quickly overtook me. I'm just one of the crew. Skipper's in charge. If we're having a discussion and he has an opinion, he has the final word."

This makes Skip smile. "The funny thing is, this would not happen in any other setting. I could tell Kjell, 'Do this,' and he would not do it. If I had a tough decision to make on the boat, I wouldn't ask for his advice because I'd have to say, 'Kjell, I'm not going to do that.'"

Kjell waves an arm. "I'm more of a daredevil. We do a lot by brawn and not by brain in Norway. Skipper would say, 'You see that fog on the horizon? Let's turn around before it engulfs us.' I would say, 'That's nothing!' When the boat heels over, he would say, 'Reef the sails.' I would say, 'Let her blow!'"

"The day Kjell buys a boat, he's the skipper, and I'll go with him," Skipper says. "If I get a life vest, he can do anything he wants."

Ed ties up the matter with a grand flourish. "Truly, truly, in any situation, the three of us look to the Skipper because we do, honest-to-goodness, have a ton of respect for him. If he doesn't have the right answer, certainly neither do we. We're ready to do what we're told."

Once the food arrives and everyone is happy with their order (though maybe not with each other's; John looks on Kjell's stew with disdain), I ask the second most pressing question on my mind. Two sides of the same coin, really. *Why sail?* was heads. Now tails: *Why this book?*

Again, they look at each other. They've never articulated this before. I am attempting to make philosophers out of an economist, a track coach, a retired retail businessman, and a student services manager on the spot.

Kjell puts everyone's thoughts into words. "I think we're documenting these sailing excursions for ourselves just as much as for our kids and grandkids. They may read them, of course, but we're not fervently insisting that they do. (If they do, I hope they think their grandpa was a cool guy who did stuff they hope to experience for themselves someday.) Speaking for me, I am grateful to have these stories written down because it gives me clarity on what's important in life and what is not. I hope that everyone gets a chance to sail at least once in their life and that it changes them the way it has me."

The truth is, for each of these men, his sailing days are numbered, and this knowledge puts a certain urgency—a high-pressurized gratitude—to preserve their adventures as they draw closer to what must soon be their final voyage. None were young on their first excursion and now fifteen years have passed. Ed had a near-fatal heart attack before ever setting foot on the boat. Even John the youngster is scheduled for back surgery to repair a herniated disc. Coming up on their sixteenth voyage, they're beginning to wonder when they should drop anchor for the last time.

"When does a man quit the sea?" asked E. B. White in *The Sea and the Wind That Blows*. "How dizzy, how bumbling must he be? Does he quit while he's ahead, or wait till he makes some major mistake, like falling overboard or being flattened by an accidental jibe?" Skipper and the crew seem to thrive pushing for the latter.

The evening ends with dark chocolate cake soaked in whiskey and crowned with warm caramel over tart whipped cream. Kjell goes falsetto at the sight. The cake is placed in the middle of the table and five spoons eagerly dive in. As we eat, I try to imagine these four characters confined in a floating container the size of a long living room, crisscrossing the slender arm of the Pacific between the US and Canada.

For these four men, the summer tradition is about much more than a boat and an ocean. Like all the best traditions, it has become greater than the sum of its parts. It is about each other and the bond created by the sheer accumulation of memories, just a few of which are in this book: sailing alongside killer whales, throwing pipes overboard Ahab-style, accidentally flying the Canadian flag upside down while coasting blithely into Victoria, running aground, debating about which sailor should get left behind when the four of them must squeeze into the three-man lifeboat (the day will surely come), saving a Catholic church from burning down, getting boarded by the US Coast Guard, losing themselves in blinding sea fog, standing rapt beneath Taps' benediction as the American flag retires in Roche Harbor.

The men begin to reminisce. I listen. I write.

To the men, to the children and grandchildren and great-grandchildren: These stories.

CHAPTER ONE
Anacortes

ὦκα δ' ἐφοπλίσσαντες ἐνήσομεν εὐρέι πόντῳ.
When that ship has been made ready
and is fit to sail,
we'll launch it out into the broad sea.

—HOMER, *ODYSSEY*

HOW IT ALL BEGAN

Ed tells the story, which begins several years before and four hundred miles east of the San Juan Islands in north Idaho's Coeur d'Alene Lake. His recitation is as clear and imposing as if he was narrating an audio book.

"For me, it's in the very beginning of *Moby Dick* where Melville talks about the ocean, the docks, the people who go to the sea: They love the boats, they love the water, they love the salt-sea air, yet they never set foot on a boat. That was me all my life in Butte where the only water you had came out of a tap that wasn't fit to drink! I've always been a lover of literature, including sailing literature; all the great sea stories were my favorite books. How about the greatest thing ever written, 'The Rime of the Ancient Mariner'?

> All in a hot and copper sky,
> The bloody Sun, at noon,
> Right up above the mast did stand,
> No bigger than the Moon.
> Day after day, day after day,
> We stuck, nor breath nor motion;
> As idle as a painted ship
> Upon a painted ocean.

I have about half of it memorized; I'm better with Hamlet. How about Macbeth? 'Out, damned spot!'"

He pauses to sip beer. If there's anything you should know about Ed, it's that everything in life connects to literature, and if there's no natural connection, he'll build a bridge, and if a bridge takes too long, he'll jump.

He gets back on track. "So when I got invited to go sailing on a little boat on Coeur d'Alene Lake with

Skipper back in the day, it was as though Christmas had come twice that year. And when I was allowed to go with them on a *real* sailing trip, it absolutely changed my life. It was opening up something to me to have that I had always wanted and never had."

Lake Coeur d'Alene—cold, blue, beautiful, shaped like a calligraphic *L*—is the body of water where Skipper learned to sail with Mark LaMoreaux, a family friend who has sailed "since he was in diapers," according to Skipper.

"I kinda inflated my résumé to get these guys to come," Skip explains. "I had no clue what I was doing. Years ago, Jan and I took the kids to Hawaii and we did one of those catamaran sunset cruises where you get food poisoning and stuff—" (Carnahan gives his washboard laugh as he pops a French fry.) "And we loved it. First time on a sailboat. Then, some time later, I spontaneously bought that beautiful little seventeen-foot sailboat for $2,000—exactly the amount I had in savings. There I was: I had a boat and I knew nothing about sailing. I called Mark and said, 'I'm in trouble. I bought a sailboat and I don't know how to sail.' Mark said, "We're going up to the lake this weekend. Bring the boat, we'll put the mast up, the sails up, the rigging up, I'll show you how to sail.'"

Every few weeks, Mark and Skipper took the boat up to Lake Coeur d'Alene and Skipper learned to sail.

Eventually he and his wife, Jan, decided they wanted to graduate to chartering a larger vessel. For that, they needed certification. So they headed northwest to Anacortes Yacht Charter to take sailing classes where basic reading, a review of important things to do or not do, and a day and a half out on the water (including overnight) was enough to get them licensed.

"That was it," Skipper says. "That was your license to charter their boat—well, actually, not *their* boat, but someone else's boat that they suckered into putting up for charter; Anacortes Yacht Charter just brokered the thing." As the one who signs the insurance papers for their own voyages, Skipper bears intense empathy for any hapless boat-owner who receives back a damaged vessel from a novice sailor. Or a non-novice sailor.

It was that cursory, two-day sailing course that set in motion the ultimate voyage.

"Here's how that came about," Ed resumes. "After my heart attack (which was in no way a catalyst, by the way; it just happened in this order), a fellow was scheduled to go on a trip with Skip and Kjell—the very first trip. But he wasn't able to go, so Skipper asked if I would come, and did I know anybody else that might blend with the three of us? I had just met John Carnahan, and though I hadn't known him very long, I was absolutely taken by his personality and the passion he had for Logos School, for his family, and all things related to the Christian life.

That's how it is, you know; you meet people along the way who build you up to the next level. So I said to the Skipper, 'How about that Carnahan guy? Have you met him?' He said, 'No, I haven't met him.' 'He seems okay to me. Let's ask him.' Skipper said, 'You ask him.' So I did. Of course I didn't know John had already sailed the seven seas and was a spoiled brat from southern California . . . "

John interrupts with a smile. "By 'sailing the seven seas,' you mean I got college credit for that boondoggle on a 555-foot old-time cruise ship. It wasn't sailing."

"So I said, 'Would you like to come on a sailing trip with us?' John said, 'Absolutely,' and the four of us became a crew. That was it." Ed raises his beer. "It was like magic."

TO ANACORTES (DEAD OR ALIVE)

Each year (traditionally the first week of June, still the off-season, though they have twice sailed in September), the men load an ample duffle bag each—nobody packs light—and cram into John Carnahan's truck for the four-hundred-mile drive to Anacortes.

At the very mention of this drive, Kjell shakes his head. Forget getting lost in fog or nearly rammed by an orca—it's the drive that should have killed these men long ago. "John's driving: insane," he says. "I think the truck makes him really feel like a man. Our trip is white knuckles all the way."

While most drivers, upon seeing signs to merge right for the upcoming exit, will actually merge right, John races stubbornly in the left lane and passes an eternity of cars until his three passengers are sure they have missed the exit; then, in the very last nanosecond, he finds room for a vehicle half their size and barges neatly in.

"It's like parallel parking at eighty miles an hour," Skipper says, who spends most of the drive calmly studying paper charts of the straits.

"John is fearless and talented behind the wheel," Ed declares. "He's the classic California driver that the Beach Boys and Jan and Dean and all of those guys sang about. He's the skipper in the truck. And *we* are not afraid."

Kjell snorts as if to say, *Speak for yourself.* "John is the personification of never being caught by the cops. Me, I think the cops park in my trunk and pop up any time I violate even the smallest rule."

To all this, John simply smiles. He is good at what he does and knows it.

Suicidal driving notwithstanding, it's true what Kjell says: The fellowship doesn't miss a beat. "The most incredible thing is that we don't really see each other a lot during the year, but we get together on this one trip and it's like nothing happened in between voyages. We pick up right where we left off."

Listening to old rock and roll stations (anything fifties, sixties, and seventies, and of course everyone knows all the lyrics—especially Ed), discussing local issues and politics, and, naturally, trashing everything Obama did, had done, would do, or wouldn't do.

"There won't be anything political to talk about in the car this year," Skip says. "Nothing's going on." (As I write this in April 2017, the Left is in a tizzy over every breath Trump has drawn since entering office. This June, if nothing else, the boys in the truck will be able to discuss how best to mass-distribute smelling salts.)

Daylight is mostly gone by the time they arrive (alive) in Anacortes. A small town on Fidalgo Island halfway between Seattle, Washington, and Vancouver, BC, Anacortes is the traditional launching point for international ferry runs and exploring the San Juan Islands, whether you join other landlubbers on a whale-watching cruise for the afternoon or charter your own vessel for a week—and anything in between.

Tradition for the crew dictates a dinner of greasy food at the Brown Lantern, a laid-back tavern and local favorite. "Seedy," Kjell says in disgust.

"It is not seedy," John says.

"It is *seedy*."

"It's just like Tapped." John gestures around the classically lit gastropub where we sit. "Except more crowded, louder, darker, more blue-collar, lots of tattoos, and sports memorabilia on the wall."

In other words, not a thing like Tapped.

After dinner, Skipper and John take a long walk with their cigars, then everyone turns in for a good night's sleep—possibly their last for a while—except Skip, who stays up to check the weather report for both skies and seas: low-pressure systems, wave height, strong currents, and so on. Weather, like the tide, varies drastically in the San Juans. Blue skies could turn to rain as quickly as a turning page. While the boat is equipped with a radio offering daily updates, Skip enjoys checking ahead. If small-craft warnings are announced, he won't sail. Such warnings have never come, but he is prepared for the day they do.

SAFEWAY SITCOM

Besides politics and music and begging John to change lanes, a major topic of conversation on the drive to Anacortes is shopping—what should they bring?—which is entertaining but pointless, as they invariably buy the same items every year.

Mid-morning before departure, Ed and John—a self-professed Abbot and Costello team—are dispatched to Safeway.

"They are bent on one mission: buying the exact opposite of what I want," Kjell complains. "If I say they should get oranges, these yahoos come back with grapefruit. When they return with grapefruit, the king of Norway gets upset."

(I agree. Grapefruit is upsetting.)

"Come on, that doesn't happen," John protests.

"*It happened last year*," insists the King. "They also use my money to buy the most foul snack food ever—pork rinds. Skipper is agnostic about this. I, the King of Norway, always howl my objections but to no avail."

Armed with their shopping guidelines, John and Ed keep fellow Safeway shoppers entertained with their tomfoolery. "Whenever people are around, it's like we're on stage," John says. "We perform. We argue like husband and wife. I'd be the husband," he adds quickly.

At the check stand, Ed regales the cashier with a gallant retelling of his life story, which John routinely interrupts to say, "Eddie, why did you get this?" "You *told* me to get that." "We don't get this kind of bread." "Well, who said we should get the cottage cheese?" Every year, the same items go on the conveyer belt and every year, the same items nearly get tossed overboard. It's all for kicks.

The food bill is split four ways, the wine and beer three because Skipper never drinks.

"It's because Carnahan brought that breathalyzer last year," Ed jokes.

I hazard a guess. Is it because he doesn't want to risk altering his judgment?

Kjell snorts: "His judgment could *use* some altering."

"It's because if he drinks, he sleeps on the spot," John says.

Truth.

Skipper explains casually, his arms folded on the table as usual: "I just didn't grow up with it, so I didn't grow up liking it. White wine makes me giddy, red wine makes me sleepy."

Another must-have is plenty of cigars, though never acquired by group shopping. ("Group-shopping for cigars would be like group-shopping for underwear," John explains.) Each man brings his own from home. And while everyone enjoys a hard drink now and then, zero liquor appears on board. "We don't want to take chances and get goofy," Ed says.

Finally, sunscreen. Skipper's reaction to wine (calm indifference) is nothing compared to Kjell's reaction to sunscreen. The stuff mystifies him as it does probably every Norwegian who grew up worshipping the rare sun.

"When the sun does come out, twice a year, people disrobe everywhere," he recalls. "They leave their offices and go out on the lawn and strip down to their underwear."

John begs, "Kjell, we just ate . . . "

"Some of them are not that bad looking," Kjell insists.

John makes a face. "That scares me, and I'm fearless!"

Shopping completed (no sunscreen for Kjell), John and Ed return to the boat with the loot. Now is time for John to prove his worth as the able-bodied youth. The fact that he is older than Kjell was at the dawn of these voyages makes no difference; he will forever be regarded as the adolescent. Two dozen bags, plus the normal luggage, pile into the loading cart which is essentially a glorified wheelbarrow, and this John maneuvers down the walkway to the dock. Depending on the tide, the walkway could be either a gentle slope or a black-diamond drop-off which leaves John digging in his heels, fighting gravity every inch, while Ed follows along supportively.

WE'RE GONNA NEED A SMALLER BOAT

"If a man is to be obsessed by something, a boat is as good as anything, perhaps a bit better than most," wrote E. B. White. Even idle in the harbor, a sailboat is "full of strange promise and the hint of trouble . . . . Here the sprawling panoply of The Home is compressed in orderly miniature and liquid delirium, suspended between the bottom of the sea and the top of the sky, ready to move on in the morning by the miracle of canvas and the witchcraft of rope."

Sailboats are indeed beautiful creatures. Even total landlubbers who know nothing of what to look for in the shape of a hull or the balance of a rig can fall in love with the sleek contours of a sailboat and feel their heart rise, as if responding to a call. Hardly anyone is immune to the promise of new horizons, the simple grace of white sails against blue sky and water.

Perhaps there are reasons why sailboats are predominantly white. Pragmatically, it might be that a white hull deflects the sun's rays and hence stays cooler inside (I've heard this point debated), plus scratches and scuffs are less visible on white (no debate there). I've also heard it said that a white boat is easier to be picked up on radar. Whatever the practical reasons, the pairing of white and blue is simply one of the world's most pleasing aesthetics. It is clouds in a cornflower sky; it is a white wedding dress with "something blue"; it is the colorscape of Alpine peaks in winter.

"No other manmade object blends design, craftsmanship, passion, and pure optimism the way a sailboat does," wrote John Kretschmer, veteran bluewater skipper in his semi-biographical book *Sailing a Serious Ocean*. "I understand why sailboats are considered feminine in most cultures. They're lovely and seductive."

With a sailboat, one feels, anything is possible.

Skipper and the crew have, almost without exception, chartered vessels through Anacortes Yacht Charters. The gaps in the timetable below represent the few times they went off-campus to other companies, but after certain mishaps—including the throttle breaking on their first day aboard a boat called *Jean-Claire*—they always return to Anacortes Yacht Charters.

Their reputation with the club has its benefits. For the first few years, they attended a mandatory safety course filled with the sort of mundane warnings that tend to insult common sense—such as "avoid shallow water"—but after proving themselves to Anacortes Yacht Charters with five responsible voyages, they acquired the elite Admiral status, a highly coveted achievement that allows them to bypass the course and head straight to their vessel. "We no longer have to grovel like the little people," Kjell says, throwing his hands regally about. "We're experienced and we have the swagger to prove it. We can communicate with the saltiest of mariners and not look like fools."

All the boats have been *sloops*: single-masted sailboats with a fore-and-aft *mainsail* (exactly what it sounds like) and a *jib* (a triangular staysail set forward of the forward-most mast). For many years, the men upgraded to steadily larger vessels: from the thirty-foot *Sunday Morning Coffee* in 1998 to the forty-six-foot *Morning Dance* in 2016. But there Skipper draws the line, much to Kjell's frustration. If any of the men have a bone of contention, it is Kjell and Skip concerning the size of the boat. Kjell, accustomed to the oceanic elbow room of his homeland's fjords, would charter a galleon if he could, but not even the King of Norway can talk Skip into maneuvering a fifty-footer.

As always, Skipper has good reason for his caution. Docking is one of the only skills the charter company truly cares about (the other being basic navigation), and long boats are extremely unwieldy in ports. For a boat, where each foot increases steering difficulty exponentially, the difference of a mere few feet feels like the difference between a mini van and a school bus.

Make	Length	Name	Dates of voyage
Catalina	30'	*Sunday Morning Coffee*	1998
Catalina	30'	*Sunday Morning Coffee*	June 2–5, 2002
Catalina	30'	*Coriolis*	June 11–17, 2005
Catalina	30'	*Coriolis*	June 10–16, 2006
Moody	41'	*Desert Wind*	June 9–13, 2007
Catalina	42'	*Solaria*	June 7–11, 2008
Bavaria	36'	*Escape*	June 6–9, 2009
Beneteau	38'	*Surprise*	June 10–13, 2009
Catalina	42'	*Solaria*	June 5–12, 2010
Catalina Mark II	42'	*A Lil R&R*	June 4–10, 2011
Catalina	42'	*Solaria*	Sept. 22–26, 2012
Bavaria	36'	*Escape*	Sept. 14–18, 2013
Beneteau	39'	*Windependent*	June 7–11, 2014
Beneteau	40'	*Pure Joy Too*	June 6–14, 2015
Beneteau	46'	*Morning Dance*	June 4–8, 2016

No matter the size, each boat has a similar floorplan and the rooms are divvied up according to esteemed tradition: the younger men honor Kjell with the large estate room and luxurious electric head in the front while John and Ed take the two smaller cabins in the back.

"I have a moment of happiness when I go into my estate room every night, and they disappear into their cubby little cabins," Kjell recalls with satisfaction. "They give me the nicest room because I'm the oldest and I'm the King of Norway." Skipper, never out of touch with his days of roughing it as a Marine, bundles up in a sleeping bag in the cockpit.

Each vessel has an important side character which one day could become the main character: the lifeboat, unalterably dubbed *Lewis* since year one. It is *Lewis*, a dinghy measuring a grand eight feet long and four feet wide, that would suddenly be in charge of bearing these men safely home should they have to abandon ship. The jest every year is, of course, which man do they sacrifice? Because the men are convinced that *Lewis* will hold only three at a time, and Kjell threatens to give the Kate Winslet treatment to any sailor unlucky enough to be clinging to the raft from the outside. "I'll never let you go!" he says, and mimes opening his fist before shaking his head. "What a liar." (Ship movies are a popular topic around the interview table. *Titanic* is ruthlessly trashed while *Master and Commander* roundly saluted and Robert Redford's *All Is Lost* basically ignored as a nonevent.)

Despite the joking, not even daredevil Kjell wishes to see the day they are forced to trade the yacht for *Lewis*. Every sailor knows that trusting your life to a lifeboat is never to be done lightly. As Kretschmer describes: "Being in a life raft is as close to hell as you can come while still being alive. It is a vessel of last resort." This truth is the reason for the old dictum that says, "Always step up into the lifeboat"—meaning your mother ship should be already down and going downer. If your vessel is even reluctantly afloat, stay on.

HELMS ALEE!

"The responsibility as skipper does weigh on me," Skip says. "I feel unease for the first twenty minutes of each cruise—not for our safety, but for the safety of the boat. I don't think others feel that. I hope they do not."

Perhaps not concern for the boat, per se, but butterflies of a different sort do visit some of the others. Even the swashbuckling Kjell approaches each sailing trip with a healthy dose of anxiety—"Probably unwarranted," he says, "but anxiety nonetheless. Things could go wrong, the weather might turn, one of us could fall overboard, and if we do, well, none of us are spring chickens any more, and it is unlikely that we would survive, especially if the weather is nasty." But this anxiety is correlated with adrenaline. "Beating the odds against all sorts of potential calamities on a boat in the ocean—now that's an adventure."

Once John the dauntless bellboy has delivered the luggage cart and the boat has been readied—all gear and provisions stowed away, the food supposedly secure (given Kjell's face, I would watch for a man-overboard grapefruit this year), and personal belongings down below—comes the great moment: shoving off.

From this time on, Skipper is entirely in charge. He fires up the motor and lets it run while the crew makes sure *Lewis*, attached to the stern by its bowline, is angled clear of the boat and out of danger of being run over when the yacht pulls backward out of the slip. There's a gust of action onboard as the men stow the electrical cord and roll up all lines tying the boat to the dock save one, released by Ed or Kjell at the last minute. They are waiting for John to spring aboard, and he is waiting on the edge of the dock to help push while Skipper runs in a careful reverse, sending smooth ripples in ribbons across the water.

It's a delicate art. The rudder needs ample water running over it in order to *bite*, or provide steerageway, so Skip must drive backward fast enough to generate this water while yet staying slow enough to maintain control in the narrow confines of the marina. John, still on the dock, pushes till Skip gives the word, then jumps aboard and Skip continues navigating at a low diesel growl through the marina's morning traffic toward the gate that opens to Guemes Channel.

Disjointed and clumsy at first, like a newly sprouted teenager with more limbs than they can control, the process of reversing out of the slip has become dexterous routine over the years. The men are on display to the entire harbor and anxious to look their best to the beverage-sipping tourists only too ready to snicker if the wind catches the boat and bumps it into a dock piling, or if the boat runs too slow for proper steerageway. Fortunately for the men's egos, they rarely have to say a word now as everyone knows their job and does it with practiced ease.

Through the gate, Skipper guides the boat out into the free water of the channel. Then he hands over the helm, usually to Ed, who turns into a happy child. "I love to drive the boat," Ed says. "Rain, snow, sleet, dark of night—I love to drive." (Never mind the fact that insurance doesn't allow night sailing; Ed already loves it in his imagination.) Skip enjoys giving Ed the helm early because, even though it took Ed about eight years to learn to steer in a straight line, he likes to see him grin. "If Ed grins," Skip says, "I know it's going to be a good day."

Their destination: whatever Skip says. Every year, the first night's stop varies depending on weather and the men's mood, but a typical voyage might begin with Friday Harbor on the northeast crook of San Juan Island. Skip simply points to a landmark—Upright Channel or Turn Island—and says, "Head for that!" That's good enough for Ed.

The real thrill comes the moment the wind picks up strong enough to hoist the sails. For Kjell, if someone so much as sneezes, there's enough breeze. At this moment Ed turns the boat into the wind and kills the motor and in the sudden reverberating silence, the men work quickly to raise the sails—the most challenging feat yet.

Sailboats are rigged with a line called a halyard which is used to pull the sails up the mast, but on the men's yacht, no halyard is necessary (in fact, "raise the sails" is something of a misnomer since no actual raising is involved) because the sails are already rolled in place inside the mast and must simply be raveled out. For this the men use a maze of color-coded ropes called *sheets*, all routed inside the cockpit, to control the mainsail and jib sail. Subtle wind calls for both sails at once so that the boat harnesses the wind's power with as much canvas as possible.

Within moments, the sails unfurl and catch the wind with the sound of snapping parachutes. Now the fun really begins. Ed begins to tack—zigzag back and forth by catching the wind first on one side of the boat, then on the other. Each zig and zag is a ninety-degree turn and calls for finely honed teamwork between Ed and at least two of the others: one manning a line on the port side, the other manning a line on the starboard, ready to let out or pull in and adjust the sail's trim as Ed turns the wheel.

And of course, everyone is keeping an eye on the boom, the horizontal pole that supports the bottom edge of the mainsail. When the boat turns, wind that was coming across the starboard side will now come across the port side, and as the wind fills the sails from this new angle, it forces the mainsail to swing like a giant canvas door on a hinge—and the boom flies. Though you would need to be about seven feet tall or standing on the seat below the gunwale to meet the boom head-on, no one wants to play chicken with what is essentially a baseball bat swung by two Babe Ruths.

The men get in position and the calls ring across the boat.

From the helm: "Ready to come about?"

From the sides: "Ready on the port!" "Ready on the starboard!"

"Helms alee!" And Ed turns the wheel.

The smooth turning of the boat belies the frenzied action on deck: sails flapping in a hellacious racket as they lose the wind, lines slapping as they are loosed or hauled, the wind swirling first this way, then that way, the boom hurtling across the wheelhouse, the windward jib line frantically tied off, the sails popping full of wind once more, then . . . silence.

After years of practice, the men can conduct a single tack in about eight seconds. About one in three times, everything goes perfectly. The other two times, the tack is followed by analysis: what went wrong, what should have been done differently, who messed up (with plenty of finger-pointing to go around). Such teamwork is one of habitual sailing's finest fruits. In Skip's eyes, this is good reason for everyone to sail at least once in their lives. "Church groups often have retreats, in part to build better people and stronger teams. I think we should take everyone sailing instead. Force us to depend on others and them on us."

The men sail in this new direction until they want to tack again, and so the boat becomes like a skier traversing a mountainside, sailing into adventure by etching gentle Zs.

"It's ancient," Ed tells me when explaining why he loves sailing. "Human beings have been sailing since God made human beings. A sail is still a sail; a boat is still a boat. We are men doing something that God gave us on almost the first page of history. It's too pure, too good, too honest."

The men are underway. The water is a deep, intoxicating blue. The only sound is of the brilliant white hull singing through the waves, a double-fanned wake streaming behind. Visible to the southwest off the port beam: the Olympic Mountains across the straits of Juan de Fuca. To the northeast and southeast almost directly off the stern: Mount Baker and Mount Rainier, twin beauties bearing snow alms to the sky. To the north off the starboard beam: the far peaks of Canada. And off the bow: the blue haze of the first of the San Juan Islands.

CHAPTER TWO

Let the Adventure Begin

Ed: In His Own Words

> Whenever I find myself growing grim about the mouth;
> whenever it is a damp, drizzly November in my soul . . .
> then, I account it high time to get to sea as soon as I can.
> —HERMAN MELVILLE, *MOBY DICK*

Sailing is the highlight of every summer. It has changed my life by giving me the chance to be a part of a group of Christian men who serve each other with friendship, sharing our lives, sharing our knowledge as we each grow in Grace, love of God and love for each other.

These adventures have been so rich that I would not feel like I was missing something if I had to stop sailing. Obviously, I wish to sail as long as I am physically able; I am keen to explore a new part of Victoria, and if the opportunity arose, I would even love to crew on a ship to England. But the past fifteen years have been gift enough. The smell of the water, the sun shining in its various, lovely angles across the boat, the ease of conversation—these memories are gold. The fact that my wife of 40 years got to sail with us twice has been wonderful, and I am profoundly grateful for the enduring friendship of the crew and the care we have for each other.

If my grandchildren and great-grandchildren happen to read these stories, I hope they have a laugh. I hope they enjoy remembering me, if they knew me. If they didn't, I hope they are reminded of the covenantal nature of families. We are all connected, even if we never met.

I owe much to the skipper, John, and Kjell. They have been so good to me.

This is year sixteen. Let the adventure begin.

CHAPTER THREE

A Day in the Life

What I want to write about today is the sea. It contains so many colors. Silver at dawn, green at noon, dark blue in the evening. Sometimes it looks almost red. Or it will turn the color of old coins . . . . It is my favorite thing, I think, that I have ever seen . . . . It seems big enough to contain everything anyone could ever feel.

—ANTHONY DOERR, *ALL THE LIGHT WE CANNOT SEE*

THE SAN JUANS

The San Juan archipelago is a scattering of forested islands stretching nearly one hundred miles in the halcyon waters north of Puget Sound. From the air, they appear to be a fractured continent, like you pounded a stake in the middle of a china plate and created instant fragments. The deepest water is impenetrable to the eye and extremely dark blue, the color of the Air Force emblem, while the islands are shrubby clusters of rich, almost shamrock green. Interrupted as they are by land masses, the straits don't smell ocean salty and never heave with typical Pacific waves, but move about like a lake playing moderately rough—perfect for undramatic sailing.

It's the temperature that could kill you. Even in summer, the water averages about fifty-two degrees—cold enough for what is known as the 50/50/50 rule: If you're in fifty-degree water for fifty minutes, you have a fifty percent chance of survival. Skipper and the crew's banter in debating who should be left hanging onto *Lewis* from the outside belies the very real danger of hypothermia in such a situation. But with benevolent seas (and the US Coast Guard a mayday call away), there's little actual danger of *Titanic* reenactments.

Plus, even at its furthest, land is always within sight, which Skip is grateful for. "We would be scared if we couldn't see land," he says, keenly conscious, as ever, of the limits of his own seamanship. "It's not that the boat wasn't meant to be that far from shore, it's that *we* weren't meant to be that far from shore."

FOUR PERSONALITIES IN A BOAT (MAN OVERBOARD!)

When it comes to the men's roles on the boat, everyone agrees that John is something of the chief documenter, taking more pictures than anybody because he is the only guy who can do more than one thing at a time. When there's physical labor to be done, he is usually the first on his feet. "John's the young guy," Kjell reasons. "He has to do most of the work. I just sit there and look regal, okay?" John is also hailed as the best educated and, save Ed, the most gifted storyteller.

Frequently the funniest and definitely the most voluble, Ed is the boat's famed raconteur, entertaining the crew with endless historical trivia, jokes, and anecdotes. He is perfectly honest when he says he can make almost anyone smile, chuckle, laugh, or—if he's lucky—fall off a bar stool. "Funny stories, dumb jokes, I can do it all. Full babble and tap dance!"

Kjell is the quietest because he naps the most, but not in his luxurious cabin with its double bed, oh no—out in the cockpit with his hat over his face and his 1936 Seiss binoculars strung around his neck, in full benediction of the sun like his good Norwegian ancestors (clothing remains put). But not because he is tired (of course not). Sleeping simply "trumps the inconvenience of being nice to the others."

Skipper is the grownup because he has to be. Despite the joshing between the men (a good deal of which coming from Skip himself), in the end, deep down, they look to Skip to keep the adventure afloat. He is discerning and preemptive, routinely rehearsing "what if" scenarios in his mind so that when the unexpected happens, it isn't unexpected. He has a plan in his back pocket and a plan B in his other pocket. This state of readiness involves everything from knowing where the life vests are stowed, to studying the charts for shallow water warnings ("I hate to admit it," Kjell says, "but Skipper is the only one who actually reads and studies those things while the rest of us feign deep knowledge of such matters"), to surprising the men with safety drills.

One such drill came on an especially wind-thrashed day when Kjell's hat—a heinously plain and universally derided baseball cap—flew off his head. Immediately, Skipper cried: "Man overboard!" He had already drilled the crew in proper safety etiquette: When someone falls off the boat, your single most important task is to keep your eye fixed on where they fell in the water. As the helmsman turns to go back and rescue them, you turn your head in sync so as to keep the swimmer fixed in your sight.

That is precisely what did not happen when Kjell's hat pitched into the sea and Skipper sounded the alarm. "I wish we had a picture," Kjell says. "As soon as Skipper said, 'Man overboard,' John looked this way, Ed looked that way, I looked the other way—Skip was the only one who kept his eye on the prize. It's like herding cats, having the three of us as a crew."

They didn't mind fumbling the drill. "It was such an ugly hat—we were glad to see it go," Ed says. "In fact, I think Ed knocked it off," Skipper adds, and Kjell agrees: "It was unbefitting a king. It's swimming with the fishes now."

As usual, what has become a laughing matter for the guys could truthfully one day spiral into a life-and-death emergency if any of the men go overboard themselves—especially given the fact that they all (even Skipper) are in the habit of enjoying the weather on deck sans the bulky life jackets.

To those with no experience, rescuing a man overboard seems simple. But to those who have attempted it even once, plucking a scared and quickly fatigued human being from the rapidly numbing water is no joke. Your chances of successfully rescuing a man overboard are actually quite small.

As you surge the boat ahead before coming about to pick them up, the swimmer becomes a near meaningless speck in the crosshatched vastness of the sea. The wind plays tricks with the sails and you are forced to quickly adjust and readjust their trim as you change directions, while the ever shifting current not only sucks the swimmer away from their initial landing place, but also foils your attempts to fling the life-preserver—assuming you're able to navigate close enough.

Such thoughts, if they do cross the men's minds, don't seem to weigh them down. Probably because every man on board really is a prudent fellow and they each put implicit faith in Skipper to ride the brakes as necessary and keep them out of serious trouble.

Skip laughs to think of it. "Their biggest mistake is trusting me. They have no idea that in any situation, the key to skippering is to say, 'It's going to be fine.' (You don't have a clue it's going to be fine; you just say that it'll be fine.) Or as a last resort: 'Hang on.'"

SALTY LANGUAGE

The men might be able to swagger with the saltiest of sailors, but they certainly don't swear like them.

Ed's parents were the decent American teetotaler type, yet language was still common in the home, so when he became a Christian he had to ready a substitute for all his favorite French. "Now I say, 'buck-tooth rabbit!' That comes out just like a cuss word." He pounds the table with satisfaction. The others look at him like he has just confessed to eating tofu instead of meat all these years. Skip says, "I have never heard you say that."

Kjell cites his pagan upbringing and says his resistance to swearing is made of weaker stuff than Ed's—and usually prompted by pain—though the others have never heard him utter a questionable word. Not even in Norwegian. Not even the time he fell from the boat onto the dock and landed straight on his hip. In his own head, he might very well have imprecated the situation in five languages at once, but aloud he cried slowly and simply: "Oh, that *really hurt*." ("What I wanted to say was something totally different," he remembers.)

Skip can thank the Marines for extending his vocabulary into unchartered waters, but those are places he never goes. Even back in the day, Ed is devoutly certain that the mild-mannered Skip did not join in. "Knowing Skipper as well as I do," he insists, "even while he was surrounded by all the colorful language humanly possible, I would bet the farm that he hardly ever, if ever, participated."

To date, the worst word ever uttered by the men on a voyage came the time Skip attempted to carry too many things while disembarking and dropped his phone into the sea—not a smartphone; a drug dealer, castaway phone; but nevertheless close to his heart—and he whispered *damn*. "Not a Marine Corps word. It could have been a lot worse."

That is very true. It could have been "buck-tooth rabbit!"

SMOKES & MUNCHIES

Much of the men's fellowship takes place around food and a good smoke (or two or three). On a lazy day—when there's no race to reach the next harbor before dark, no great wind to harness, and time is a gentle master—both eating and smoking start early. Breakfast is usually eaten on board around 9:00, after which John and Ed handle dishes. Skip usually manages to dodge them by "studying" charts and "checking" the oil, and Kjell avoids them by falling asleep under his hat.

Mid-morning, John and Skip break out the cigars. "You have to get an early start if you want to get through three a day—though three a day would be unheard of on dry land," says Skip.

He adds a note on the important attitude of disciplined freedom with such pastimes. "We don't throw restraint to the wind; the point is that the very things I grew up regarding as vices we have learned to enjoy as blessings: a good wine, a fine cigar, etc. I hope my kids and grandkids recognize that the real issue is to enjoy these gifts as gifts, without flaunting them or letting them control you. Sure, we smoke and drink, but it's always under control and it's all good and pleasing to the Lord."

For Skip, cigars are like soda: They last forever. What John can smoke in 30 minutes, Skip will stretch out over an hour and fifteen minutes until it seems the widow who ministered to Elijah will run out of oil and flour before Skip runs out of cigar.

This frustrates Kjell to no end. "Skip is an absolute basket case in two things," he says at the interview table, raising his beer. "One, this beer right here would last him about two days, and two, he refuses to light a cigar. I've been observing him (when I'm not asleep). He lights about one-fourth, sucks on it violently, looks at it again, then sucks on it some more. You're supposed to light the whole thing!"

In the willful way of kings, Kjell cares an awful lot about Skip and his cigars despite the fact that he himself hates smoking. He once tried one of John's cigars—an experiment that displeased him greatly. "If you're going to smoke, you might as well inhale it down to your toes, and that's what I did." He shudders. "The taste stayed with me for two days."

Ed used to enjoy both pipe and cigar, but has recently wimped out for reasons similar to Kjell's. "They're too hard on me. Besides, pipes smell better than they taste, and cigars taste better than they smell. I'm not missing much." He even choreographed his own pipe-dismissal ceremony one fine sunny morning when he discovered a crack in his pipe bowl. Taking up position at the helm, he threw the thing overboard with a glorious sweep of the arm while John recited the famous pipe scene in *Moby Dick*, as near as he could from memory after having taught it to tenth graders at Logos School.

> "How now," he soliloquized at last, withdrawing the tube, "this smoking no longer soothes. Oh, my pipe! hard must it go with me if thy charm be gone! Here have I been unconsciously toiling, not pleasuring—aye, and ignorantly smoking to

windward all the while; to windward, and with such nervous whiffs, as if, like the dying whale, my final jets were the strongest and fullest of trouble. What business have I with this pipe? This thing that is meant for sereneness, to send up mild white vapors among mild white hairs, not among torn iron-grey locks like mine. I'll smoke no more." He tossed the still lighted pipe into the sea. The fire hissed in the waves; the same instant the ship shot by the bubble the sinking pipe made. With slouched hat, Ahab lurchingly paced the planks.

For Ed, to be the hero of one of his favorite literary works—even for a moment—was a fine adventure indeed. The dramatization was captured on video and he is quite pleased to this day that you can hear the tiny splash. "And I haven't had a pipe since," he declares.

After the morning cigars, it's about 11:00 when John looks around the boat. The most active crewmember, he is eager to find an excuse to get something done. "Is it too early for lunch?" Acclamation all around. So John heads down into the saloon and prepares sandwiches (bologna and cheese for three; deli beef for the King), potato chips, pickles, carrot sticks (so they can tell their wives they ate well), and a beer each (Diet Pepsi for Skipper). If they've been running the engine, they cut it off now and let the boat drift. Without the motor drone, the world turns abruptly tranquil and the water's faint salt smell strengthens, free of the sharp tinges of diesel.

Now is the time for philosophizing. "There's no better environment on the planet for unfettered thinking than a boat at sea," according to Kretschmer in *Sailing a Serious Ocean*. Talk radio, current affairs, historical events, movies, theology . . . "And naturally, we say absolutely wonderful, exceptional things about our wives," says Ed. He isn't joking. And every tenth of June, they use precious cell phone minutes to place a long-distance call to Kjell's wife, Judi, and sing happy birthday.

For dinner, John and Ed are the popular chefs and have worked up a number of gourmet winners: fried steaks, chicken, spaghetti, salmon, meat and potatoes. But nothing beats Kjell's chili, everyone's favorite traditional meal. Not a year has gone by without chili day. "I am the local hero because it is always better this year than last year," Kjell says. "My wife equips me with the secret sauce—a jar of unknown spices, for which I always take full credit."

And Skip? He doesn't cook. "I'm the skipper. There are certain rules. Skippers don't cook."

Dinner dishes after chili day are their own shebang. By this time the men have reached their harbor for the night, and while Skip and Kjell stroll the docks, John cues up the Bobby Vinton station on Pandora and he and

Ed bustle along to the custard-smooth fifties hits. It's the Safeway sitcom all over again: singing, laughing, chiding ("Look at this spoon! I can't dry that dirty thing!") until somehow the dishes get done.

8.5 KNOTS

"There is no more thrilling sensation I know of than sailing," wrote Jerome K. Jerome in his famed travelogue *Three Men in a Boat*. "It comes as near to flying as man has got to yet—except in dreams."

Perhaps the best part of a day on the water is reaching top speed. At such times John can usually be found standing with one arm wrapped around the jib in the very tip of the bow, where he is the first to break the wind and any swell of the water feels like the boat is in liftoff. "Like you're on a merry-go-round, only making headway."

The bow is also Skipper's favorite spot, whenever he isn't steering. As for Ed and Kjell, they prefer the cockpit and both are reasonably trustworthy helmsmen, though Ed might still occasionally go in circles and Kjell might still push the boat too hard. "Needing to go fast on the water is a Norwegian thing," Skipper claims.

That may be, but boys are boys, and the truth is they all like to sail as fast as they can; they simply have different definitions of *can*. For Skipper, *can* is *should*. For Kjell, *can* is *we'll survive*. In a strong wind, nautical prudence dictates that you reef the sails. Reducing sail won't knock off your speed so much, but it will improve your control since it lessens the boat's heel. But such a wind whips Kjell into the same feisty three-year-old who chucked a rock at a Nazi soldier during the German invasion of Oslo. "Let's do it!" he'll cry, shoulders up and fists pumping like he's about to take on the ocean in a fist fight. Full sail. He holds the record of eight and a half knots—almost ten miles an hour—while Skip himself has been known to bust up to eight, tops. Any faster and he fears losing the mast.

Truly, what would be crawling in a car is racing on the water. Combine the boat's motion with the current (picture yourself sprinting down a moving walkway in the airport) and you are soaring. But even Kjell admits, "In really strong winds, you've got to be on your game," and that's when Skip takes the helm. With its deep and heavy keel, the yacht is built to heel until the gunwale is level with the water, though such a maneuver keeps you on your toes—in both senses. On a deck pitched at forty-five degrees, where do you stand? The helmsman must also know when to steer into the wind and when to fall off, and "The only one good at that is Skipper," says Kjell. "None of the rest of us could be trusted at the helm in that kind of weather."

DOCKING DANGERS

The men raise Friday Harbor late the first afternoon. As they approach, Skipper gets on the radio to request a slip. "Friday Harbor, Friday Harbor, this is sailing vessel *Windependent*. Over."

For years, Skip loathed the radio. Protocol prescribes certain words in a certain order, and he feared jumbling them up or not being able to hear the harbor's reply. Just like trimming your sails or tacking, your radio prowess can prove you a veteran . . . or the lack thereof instantly betray you as a green sailor. "You might very well be a bumbling idiot, but you don't want to sound like it," Skipper says. His secret to handling the radio now is to simply pause and gather his thoughts. "They'll just think your boat is sinking and you've got to handle it and you'll be back in a minute."

Once he receives confirmation from the harbor, he continues: "We're looking for a slip for the night, bow in. We're thirty-nine feet long. Over." He always requests to dock bow in (facing the harbor) because he refuses to back into a slip. "Not gonna happen. Sorry."

The three crew members enjoy maintaining command of the helm for as long as possible as they enter the harbor, "feigning expertise in case anybody is watching us through binoculars," recalls Kjell. "We stand there looking a little bit arrogant, very loose with the wheel, because we know Skipper is about to take over."

If pulling away is dicey, coming in is even more so. "Putting that baby to bed at night is dangerous," Ed says—for everyone except perhaps the King. Rather than making sternway into free water, Skipper must pull in right up to the dock, slow enough not to ram the pilings but fast enough to maintain steerageway, all the while negotiating with the current.

Then comes the riskiest part for John and Ed, one jumping off the bow and the other off the stern down onto the dock to tie off the boat. The slightest miscalculation could end in serious injury: catching a foot on the rail and pitching headfirst, trapping a leg between the boat and the dock, or simply misjudging the distance and landing on unsuspecting ankles. "It's getting a little harder for me, though I'm capable in a tough spot," Ed says. "Fifteen years is a long time. There's a huge difference between fifty and sixty-five."

So far, the worst luck has befallen John. More precisely, John's trousers. Once, he fell onto the dock and put a rip in brand new pants. "We heard about that story for the next three trips!" Ed recalls. Another year, John leaned against a tar-covered piling and slapped the black, treacly stuff neatly on the back of his jeans—again, brand new. "I had to put them in the work pile," he remembers. "Those jeans exfoliated tar for weeks!"

CHAPTER FOUR

Friday Harbor

> Simply sailing in a new direction,
> you could enlarge the world.
>
> —ALLEN CURNOW

WELCOME TO FRIDAY HARBOR

If Friday Harbor was any man personified, it might be Kjell: a charming, pint-sized village with big personality and rich history. Tucked beside a small peninsula on the east side of San Juan Island, the picturesque little place is a common destination for ferries from Anacortes and a popular launching point for whale-watching tours.

Turn-of-the-century wood-frame houses and red, green, or yellow shops with white trim decorate the waterfront. Docks the color of great blue herons lean on long, spindly pilings. The marina teems with ranks of anchored sailboats, their bare poles bristling like flocks of white church steeples in the cobalt water. The boats range from simple fishing boats, to Friday Harbor's famous two-masted wooden schooner *The Spike Africa*, to multi-million-dollar mega yachts.

Getting off the boat inaugurates a prank show featuring Ed and Skip as surprisingly expert con artists, Kjell as passive star, and John as innocent-eyed corroborator. The audience and unwitting butts of the joke: anyone who happens to pass by.

"Something happens to Ed and Skipper on the boat," Kjell says. "As soon as we reach harbor, all bets are off."

Normally restrained and polite and "civilized," the two transform into uncontrollable extroverts: one the party, the other the life of the party, targeting strangers on the docks and making instant (if baffled) friends.

"Bolder than anybody I've ever seen," Kjell describes. "And they invariably introduce me as the King of Norway." Which folks believe—especially when Kjell greets them in Norwegian. Flummoxed, folks now aren't sure whether to bow or curtsy or kiss his hand, but their discomfort is short-lived because Ed and Skip are already moving on to the next band of commoners.

With a considerable wake of dazed and dazzled pedestrians thus established, the men head to dinner. Herb's Tavern is a favorite. The cheerful tavern is loud and laid back, crowded with pool tables and sports screens, smelling of stale beer and fried seafood and disinfectant. It was here that the men watched President Reagan's state funeral in California on June 7, 2004.

ED'S EXPERIMENTAL EATS

Ed has saved some of his best antics for Friday Harbor, all self-inflicted but some against his will. Two have involved food. Well, sort of.

Friday Harbor was the first stop on Ed's pioneer voyage—probably not the best introduction to coastal bathroom facilities. He found himself in a "nasty, dusty little place" where he wanted to brush his teeth as quickly as possible. Get in, get done, get out. He reached into his shaving kit, grabbed the toothpaste, gifted his toothbrush with a goodly amount, and started brushing.

At first he tasted nothing different.

Then he looked down and saw, in his hand, the hydrocortisone.

Another fellow entered the facilities just in time to see Ed lose it. "Bleh, bleh, bleh!" trying to spit hydrocortisone out of his mouth and splash water into his mouth at the same time.

Wordless, the stranger angled himself to the sink furthest away possible.

"I was a total, goofy-looking mess," Ed remembers. "Hydrocortisone absolutely was not meant to be tasted or imbibed." He vacated the bathroom as fast as he could and dashed back to the boat and upended a bottle of wine for a few good swigs and rinses, which probably didn't cleanse his palate, but did help his spirits regain some equilibrium.

Then there's the ice cream story, which everyone regards as a debacle except Ed. He is a man of great common sense except in a few areas. One of those is hating ice cream. "It's illegal," Kjell says. "I'm the King and I say it is absolutely illegal not to like ice cream."

What should Friday Harbor have but a popular ice cream shop offering an edible anthology of hand-dipped goodness. One trip, Ed spontaneously declared, "Fine, I'll have ice cream. I'll have that," and pointed.

If anything could offend an ice cream fanboy more than refusing to partake, it's partaking of licorice flavor. Ice cream, like snow, has no business being black.

"Eddie, that's licorice!" John cried. "You don't want that."

"Yes, I do. I'm going to have ice cream and I'm going to have that."

Moments later, Ed was grinning happily, stained black around the lips, licking away. He looked like he had tried to kiss tar. "This isn't so bad!"

Skip shakes his head. "I think he always liked ice cream. He was just being stubborn."

THE OLD-TIMERS AND THE CANNON

One year as the men walked the docks into Friday Harbor's downtown, a thrilling and gigantic KAPOW concussed the air. Echoes rocketed across the harbor, shattering on Jones Island half a mile away.

The men looked up. There, on top of the shrub-covered hill rising gently above the harbor, two old men—if not three sheets to the wind, at least one or two—were jumping around in a shower of sparks. Behind them: the American Legion building. In front of them: an old ceremonial cannon which, until a minute ago, had been filled with gunpowder. And below them: a hill suddenly on fire. Dry brush snapped into flames the size of a large bonfire.

Just as quick were the sounds of sirens pealing through town. By the time the sailors reached the main road, firetrucks were wailing up the hill to rescue the up-and-coming arsonists from their little inferno.

"It was pretty neat, how quickly the fire department responded," the men remember. Which is probably code for wishing *they* had been the old-timers trying to set the town on fire.

FOGBOUND

Skipper isn't afraid of much, but if he loathes anything, it's fog. "Fog is an unfriendly hug," he says. "It is the wrong guy in your personal space. It is bad breath, bad manners, and poor character in one package. Wind you can manage, waves you can ride, but fog is the one thing you dread seeing."

It was early morning on the last day of this particular voyage, and what should the men see but fog moving in off the water, steadily erasing the world and hanging over the town like a wet, diseased towel. Where it stayed.

Friday Harbor is frequently the men's first and final stop, and today, they needed to do just one thing: sail the clear shot back to Anacortes. Except that in fog, it is anything but a clear shot. The men debated what to do. This was their last day with the boat. They had to get home. "Stay put till the fog clears," advised Anacortes Yacht Charters.

An hour later, the fog began pulling back, so the sailors decided to give it a go. It was a bait and switch. Barely a quarter mile out, the fog regrouped, solid as a pale stone wall. Skipper motored slowly. It was an eerie world. Very little wind stirred. Blindness and deafness, converted to color, would share the same sickly shade smearing water and horizon and sky together into one porous curtain. Fog dampens sound; the water droplets in the air attenuate and disperse the sound waves, so that the only thing the men could hear was the murmur of their own motor and the slurping of the sea against the hull.

Skipper couldn't see a thing until, suddenly—a glow ahead. He had fallen behind a powerboat. For a while he followed the light, but the powerboat was sailing a knot faster and soon melted back into the oblivion.

That was enough. The men turned back.

After another hour in port, they decided to try again. By now it was mid-morning and the fog was still thick. But as they sailed, the fog withdrew in front of them, allowing Skipper to see just a few feet at a time. For more than twenty miles, the boat parted fog and water together till the men arrived safely in Anacortes. Sighs of relief passed around the boat.

"It was a long haul," Kjell remembers. "I had moments of goose bumps and moments of feeling clammy. Three hours is a long time to be caught up in something you shouldn't have been."

CHAPTER FIVE

Like Old Friends Shaking Hands

John: In His Own Words

> It must be remembered that the sea is a great breeder of friendship. Two men who have known each other for twenty years find that twenty days at sea bring them nearer than ever they were before, or else estrange them.
>
> —GILBERT PARKER

To think that we have been doing this fifteen years! Our first trip seems a lifetime ago. We were all so young (well, three of us were). Sailing always makes me think of Ratty in *The Wind and the Willows*. "There is nothing, absolutely nothing, quite so wonderful as messing about in boats." You don't know how true that is until you've tried it.

In some ways mirroring a marriage, the trip has evolved from being completely new—each movement, decision, event having to be thoroughly vetted—to being nearly completely comfortable (if that's the word); repeated decisions made by rote, events reoccurring like old friends shaking hands at a reunion. Of course there are new things each trip, but they are now more like salt and pepper: adding flavor and variety, but never changing the heart of the meal.

I think of coming about, either tacking or jibing. We've really grown in this maneuver. We are now a finely honed machine. It doesn't matter who is at the helm or who is manning the port or starboard lines; it has become a beautiful thing.

The camaraderie—that is what I am most grateful for. Sailing has given me some of my best friends and also allowed me to see parts of the world I wouldn't have seen otherwise. It has been a blessing in my life, and I am excited to pass on the stories. I hope that through these anecdotes—just snatches of memories, really—my kids and grandkids gain further insight into who I am, and who I was.

Helms alee!

CHAPTER SIX
Victoria

I'll come back for you
From across the ocean blue;
Carried on the back of a whale
With feathers sown together
To make a big white sail.
—SAMUEL RUDYARD DICKISON, "ELEPHANTS"

THE UGLY STEPSISTER

"Sidney!" Ed growls the name like it was cheap whiskey.

Skip shakes his head. "Bad option. Sidney is bland. Let's not go there."

"There's no bar where you can go and have a Long Island," Kjell complains.

"It's this nothing port," John says, mediocre words failing him. "It's like . . . whatever."

Sidney, sitting on the final eastern shreds of Vancouver Island, just across the Salish Sea from Vancouver itself, was an overnight stop on two of the earlier voyages. The men docked the boat, rented a car, and drove south to the real destination: Victoria. The contrast between the two British Columbian ports could hardly have been more in Victoria's favor.

"Sidney is like going to Lewiston when you could go to Coeur d'Alene," John says.

Skip adds, "If Victoria is a banana split, Sidney is low-cal vanilla yogurt." He was especially unimpressed with the layout of the harbor. To reach their slip, he navigated their forty-odd-foot sailboat through a labyrinth of tight corners into the very heart of the marina—only to discover the slip was built for a twenty-foot vessel. "It was like Cinderella's step-sisters and the glass slipper," he says. "You *wanted* it to fit, but you just can't pretend that it did."

"The port didn't fit and it was just about as ugly!" Ed declares.

Two trips was all it took for the men to decide to avoid Sidney and sail southwest from Roche Harbor (a common first stop, along with Friday Harbor) directly to Victoria—which they do now nearly every year. It's a more adventurous route because they bisect the wide shipping lanes of Haro Strait for nearly the entire passage of twenty-two and a half nautical miles (twenty-six landlubber miles).

With the nearest US island several miles east and Canada another several miles west, cutting down the strait takes them the furthest they ever sail from land. More water to cross simply means more opportunities for anything to go wrong. Engine problems, rough seas, ruthless fog, ferries and hulking freighters who own the right of way by right of size alone are just a few of the obstacles that might turn a normal four-hour passage into the sort of thrill that would make even Kjell wish for dry land.

Naturally, of all the routes, Roche to Victoria receives Skipper's sharpest attention. He gives the charts extra focus and always budgets two days for Victoria in case they need to stay in the harbor a second night while foul weather passes. But once again, the crew is unconcerned. They know their skipper is handling it. "Skip's always very cautious going into the strait," Kjell says. "He studies water depths, winds, waves, turns. We say, 'Whatever.'"

The hazards don't let up when they near Victoria. An international port, Victoria flows with ferries, water taxis, seaplanes propelling low, commercial tugs and barges, fishing fleets, whale-watching cruises, kayaks, and of course, sailboats. Bright red, yellow, or green buoys dot the watery highway to guide traffic as the men sail around the craggy southern end of Vancouver Island and up around into Victoria's inner harbor, carving the tail of a large, sweeping J.

Victoria's beauty makes the longer passage and hectic port worth it. The stately capital of British Columbia was marketed as "a little bit of Old England" by real estate agents to none other than Rudyard Kipling. He promptly contradicted them. "No England is set in any such seas or so fully charged with the mystery of the larger ocean beyond," he wrote.

The master wordsmith tried to capture Victoria with various descriptions, and felt like he failed. "I tried honestly to render something of the color, the gaiety, and the graciousness of the town and the island, but only found myself piling up unbelievable adjectives, and so let it go with a hundred other wonders . . . . Amongst all the beautiful places in the world, and I think I have seen the most beautiful of them, Victoria ranks the highest."

Victoria's inner harbor is a palatial scene with its wide, curving wall, its neo-baroque Parliament Buildings—Salzburgesque with their fair-stoned facades and emerald domes—and the Empress, a rich brick castle of a hotel wherein Edward Prince of Wales once waltzed in the Crystal Ballroom in 1919.

The men have various reasons for loving Victoria. Kjell enjoys getting there even more than being there, because "sailing through the strait with the big open water is the closest thing we have to the real ocean."

"Victoria has the most international flavor of any west coast city," Ed says. "Much more international than Seattle, Portland, or San Francisco. The flavor of the place is rooted in an incredible history. You see people from all over the world. You'd have to go down to the Farmers Market in LA to run into that many different people."

"I'll tell you why we go to Victoria," Skip says. "It's because we're the manliest guys in town."

John agrees. "It's this soft, safe, cosmopolitan, liberal place ('Lots of liberals,' Kjell interjects with distaste) and we feel like we're John Wayne in *El Dorado*, walking in with spurs and cowboy hats. We sit down and they say, 'Would you like a sparkling water?' And we say, 'No, give me a Long Island!'"

Once they've made port, the guys join Victoria's festive downtown area near the marina. Milestones, a smart-looking, energetic bar and grill overlooking the harbor, is a common destination for drinks, munchies, and people-watching. Long Islands acquired, the sailors sit outside where they can survey everything going on. "All the happening happens right there," Ed says.

The three tobacco enthusiasts sometimes pop into Old Morris, a luxurious tobacconist (one of Canada's oldest) self-branded for wealthy entrepreneurs and young culture hawks. From the alabaster and leaded-glass archway to the gallery-shaped interior gleaming with mahogany, marble, and onyx, Old Morris is as High Victorian as it gets.

"A man-cave store," John describes. "Humidors, Cuban cigars, dark wood, glass-doored cabinets . . . "

Kjell just rolls his eyes. "It means absolutely nothing to me. It's special to these guys."

"It's a snooty place," Skip says. "Their noses go up as soon as we walk in."

The only item the crew ever bought was a Cuban cigar for Skipper as a thank-you gift—which he made sure to smoke over Canadian waters so that it didn't wind up with the same soggy demise as one of John's cigars (a story that will have to wait).

O CANADA

One year, the men were tacking back and forth on a brawny wind, preparing to enter the harbor, when Skipper suggested, to honor their foreign hosts: "Let's hoist the Canadian flag." Kjell hopped to. He hooked the flag to the main mast and hoisted it high in the air where the white and blood-red flag curled open on the wind.

The maple leaf was waving on its head. The flag was upside down.

The King of Norway clutched his fluffy white head, aghast. Sealing the flag's topsy-turvy fate was the fact that the loop in the line had come undone and the flag was stuck at the top of the mast forty feet high. No way to pull it down. A yoyo on a broken string.

"My heart sank," Kjell says. "It was an honest mistake, but I felt terrible."

All Skipper said was: "We *cannot* go into harbor with that flag upside down."

So John and Ed rigged a human contraption. After they managed to coax the flag down a few more feet, Ed braced himself against the mast because he was the sturdiest, though he claims it was because he was "dumb enough to do it." John, the spryest, stood on Ed's shoulders and, armed with the boat hook telescoped to full length, went fishing for Canada.

"I was not invited to the team," Kjell remembers plaintively.

Ed, over six feet, John, another full six feet, plus the valiant if fairly unwieldy boat hook barely snagged the loop and pulled the distressed maple leaf back down. They reconnected the loop, flipped and rehoisted the flag, and sailed proudly into harbor. Swagger regained.

IGNORED AT THE STICKY WICKET

One year, the men sought dinner at the Sticky Wicket, a cricket-themed pub sprawling over multiple levels and glaringly lit with hockey games on large TV screens. Half an hour went by while the men sat on a bench at the entrance, waiting in vain for the host to notice and seat them. The entire time, who should make the interlude more pleasant but an outrageously inebriated young man who elbowed in, sat down, and proceeded to jabber their ears off.

"He talked more vociferously than *I* do," Ed exclaims. "Pretty blasted and a little belligerent and *very* annoying. He was one of those borderline guys where one minute, he might leave, the next, he might be swinging fists. He had that tension."

"Kjell would have fought him," John says. "Kjell's our fight guy. He's the champ."

Kjell says drily, "I'm just bait."

"Cannon fodder," Skip agrees.

When the men (sans the drunk) finally scored a table, they waited yet another half an hour while multiple orbiting servers steadily avoided eye contact. No menus. No drinks. No be-right-with-yous.

"They literally didn't want to do business with us and I don't know why," Ed cries. He's getting worked up now, just thinking about it. "They were doing business with shadier-looking people who came in *after* us."

If Ed didn't exactly go postal, he certainly talked a little faster than usual and said a little less than usual. He vented for the entire group. "We didn't have to sin because he was sinning for all of us," John says with a grin.

"I was rambling on in an unhappy matter," Ed admits, "while these fellows were being patient like you're supposed to. Eventually they squared me away. That's one of the reasons I'm so grateful for these trips. I've learned so much from these guys. They regularly, but in a gentle way, broaden my Christian horizons."

Just before the last trumpet sounded and history came to an end, the sailors said "forget it" and ditched the restaurant in favor of Smith's Pub. There they ran into a congenial young man who ended up sitting and talking with them during a successfully waitered dinner. Throughout the evening, it became obvious that the kid was not a believer, so after shaking hands and parting ways, Ed, thinking he would conduct himself as a wonderful Christian man, suggested to the others on the walk back to the boat: "Fellows, let's pray for that really nice guy at the pub."

Skipper added, "And how about that guy who was a pain in the butt at the Sticky Wicket?"

Ed nearly withered on the spot. But he bit the bullet and prayed for the drunk.

RUNNING AGROUND (AND FREE HUGS)

If you ask the men for the worst moment out of fifteen years of sailing, they will point to the bone-jarring shock they had one year while entering Victoria.

"It was the apex nightmare," Skipper says. He was at the helm on a finely dressed afternoon—benevolent blue skies, cool winds gracing the air, the water an agreeable friend—while the boat cruised slow and easy toward the busy channel that led into the harbor. They were about to rub shoulders with dozens of other craft (both water and air) and the traffic signs were just as busy as the traffic. To help Skipper, the crew kept sharp eyes out for directions on where to go.

A large sign glared from wooden piling: STAY RIGHT OF YELLOW BUOYS, then, in a classic act of *do as I say, not as a do*, pointed to the left. Everyone deduced that this meant they should steer left, but keep to the right side of the piling.

Skipper turned to port.

For a few moments, all went well.

BOOM. The boat rocked violently. The stern popped several feet out of the water, knocking everyone airborne and throwing Ed out of his seat on the gunwale. For a few seconds, everyone was stunned.

Though it had never happened before, Skip knew immediately: they had collided with a submerged rock. His first thought was *Where's the best place to sink?* Scrambling to his feet, he demanded: "Are we taking in water?"

John hurried down into the saloon to check. No water came gushing in, but as far as they knew, they were still far from dandy. A blow that fierce could have damaged the prop or thrashed a series of smaller breaches in the hull that would only show up later in a slow swamping of the boat's hold or engine compartment.

If you've blown a tire while driving seventy miles an hour, or your plane has suddenly dropped a few hundred feet in the middle of a smooth flight, then you have some idea of the jump it gives your heart to have your boat go from gliding along to ramming its six-ton weight—the equivalent of three SUVs—into rocks hiding beneath the surface.

"The suddenness, the unexpectedness, the shudder, the loud noise all happening simultaneously to all four of us, and not knowing for just those few seconds what the heck had happened, but knowing it was something really bad . . . " Ed's eyes are wide as he remembers. "You have to get your act together, and the skipper did. We all fell in behind him. He said what we needed to do and we did it; we didn't even talk about it."

Everything was done quickly and calmly. The boat was seized with an energy and a hyper focus unlike any before. The men felt no fear, panic, or even mad rush of adrenaline. They were aggressively engaged. "You don't go waste time wondering, *How could this happen? What if it's a total disaster?*" John says. "You just think, *Okay, I'm in this situation; what's the next thing?*"

Skipper shut down and restarted the engine to make sure it could still run. He tested the steerage. He moved the boat forward and backward, checking the propeller. As soon as he felt like they had control (still with no idea of the extent of the damage below), he motored straight to see if they were taking on water.

"The first emotion I had wasn't fear, it was feeling bad for the guy who owned the boat," Skipper remembers. "We weren't in danger of drowning; we could have stood on top of a sunk boat. I just didn't know how bad the boat had been damaged. Since I knew there was no good outcome, I was wondering, *What's the* least *harm it might have done?*"

"Hitting a rock is the thing you've been avoiding the entire trip," John explains. "Even paying $90 a day in insurance, you're still in a $300K-$500K boat that isn't yours!"

A harbor police approached in his single-man runabout and yelled: "Hey, you guys hit a rock. Move to your port!" Skipper complied and at length safely docked the boat in Victoria's inner harbor, where he contacted the charter company. The men had planned to be joined by their wives for the second half of the trip. Of all the boats in all the years, this boat must be safe.

Anacortes Yacht Charters was remarkably unperturbed about the entire situation. "Keep sailing," they said. "Just use your good judgment and we'll check it out once you return to Anacortes."

The irony of word choice was not lost on Skipper. "We'd just crashed the boat," he says. "No one should have asked that we use our 'good judgment' for anything related to boating or navigation."

After docking the injured vessel, the sailors walked into downtown Victoria to the Sticky Wicket, where this time they were not ignored, nor was there a pestiferous boozer. They sat outside on the sundeck and quietly drank their beer. The incident had put them in a bit of gloom. What Skipper said was true: The worst part wasn't the scare—they would not have drowned—but the simple fact that after all these years, they had finally done what no sailor wants on their record: run aground. In someone else's boat.

After a while, what should come walking down the street but a little horde of friendly folks offering free hugs. Ed spied this as an opportunity to cheer everyone up. "They were some delightful and, I might say, very attractive young people," he relates, which makes the other men snort. "A young lady walked close by and said, 'We're giving free hugs; would anyone like a free hug?' She was about college age."

John widens his eyes. "I thought she was in her fifties."

"She was really needy," Kjell grumps. "And *super* liberal."

Ed elbows his way back into his story. "So to pull us out of the tailspin we were in" (cue John's washboard laugh, the incredulous version) "I said, 'Sure, I'll take a hug.'"

But instead of the young lady, a young man (who was almost as good-looking) came up and wrapped his arms around Ed. Ed returned the hug and said bravely, "Hey, thanks." The kid said, "Thank *you*." Ed proceeded to look at the lady. She said, "Thanks," and moved on down the street.

"That's my free hug—I hugged a man," Ed says sadly, while the others just laugh and shake their heads. "But the worst part of the entire scene was that we thought Skipper—having just hit a rock—would be in the doldrums, so we bought him all these shots to brighten his day, but he remembers everything with crystal clarity. He didn't drink! He wasn't in the doldrums after all! What a waste. No, we didn't buy him any shots," Ed reverses without pause. "Skip never drinks. I'm just talking." (A classic Ed fish story.)

"I wasn't in the doldrums," Skip says calmly. "If we had been sitting there drinking beer, watching our boat sink, I *might* have been. I was just full of sympathy for the boat owner. I couldn't think of anything else."

"When Skip is 'full of sympathy,' he gets focused and very quiet," John describes. "Measured in his speech—even more measured than usual."

"The moment we ran aground, we had been revering John Sawyer the Skipper, masterful helmsman," Kjell explains. "He proceeded to make a mistake and his world came apart. He was not necessarily at fault for this (we were all reading the signs), but he perceived himself to be because the buck stops with him."

The shared adrenaline on board now turned to shared resolution not to let the mishap get them down. "It wasn't a good deal, but it's part of what we're doing, and we're not going to let it mess us up," Ed told the others. And it didn't. The mistake could have hung over them and affected their judgment, certainly their mood, for the rest of the trip, but they refused to let it.

A SAILOR AND TRUE CAPTAIN

When the sailors sailed back to Anacortes to pick up their wives a few days later, a diver hired by the yacht charter swam under the boat to assess the hull. Running aground had struck the boat's keel—essentially a flat blade sticking down into the water at the bottom of the hull and the boat's lowermost structure. The keel is the first feature you measure to determine how shallow you can sail.

The rock, the diver told Skip, had knocked off flakes of white fiberglass coating, but the keel was not punctured, making the boat safe enough for the second voyage. After the couples returned, the boat would be out of commission for the season to undergo repairs.

Skipper didn't feel so bad for the owner once he knew the damage had been relatively slight, and that while the owner would be boatless during the summer, he would at the end of it receive a completely refurbished vessel, covered by insurance.

"The reason we hit the rock was because there were no red dots on the chart, marking shallow water," Skip recalls. "Usually those red dots tell you places to avoid. Of course," he adds, "a million boats go into Victoria every year and we were the only ones who hit ground. It's kind of on us."

Skip, as ever, assumes responsibility like a true captain. As for hitting the rock, he stands in good company, because as Kretschmer claims, "You're not a sailor until you go aground."

THE FREIGHTER IN THE FOG

Around year seven, fog hounded the men once again. But not in harbor. This time, they were sailing south toward Victoria, still several hours from making port, with no option of staying safely on land when the fog set in.

The day began sunny. The only concern to watch was the Canadian sea lane on their starboard side where giant oil tankers and container ships the size of sideways skyscrapers powered through the water, their bulk hiding their true speed of fifteen to twenty-five knots—many times that of the yacht. A wide berth is the only thing to be given vessels of this size.

"When you're up against a freighter, it doesn't matter how close you are," John says. "*You move.* It wouldn't even know if it hit you."

"You don't exist," Ed adds. "You're not even a bug on the windshield."

Small boats must also avoid sailing between any freighter and its seagoing tug. The two can be separated by enough space for you to easily cross between, but they are connected by a three-inch steel cable several hundred feet long, whose slack can sag into the water and strangle your propeller, or remain high and taut where it clotheslines your mast. A cable once sliced an unsuspecting water skier in half.

On this day, the men were a safe distance away from the sea lane when a fog bank appeared off the bow. Behind was clear blue sky, so the men assumed the fog was burning off and they should continue forward. But instead of disintegrating to wisps parted easily by the yacht's prow, the fog thickened and encircled the boat, sealing it off from the world. The men were completely caged in whiteness and silence. Beyond the bow, they could see nothing.

Everyone tensed up. They were all thinking about freighters in the sea lane. The GPS, on which they appeared as nothing more than a tiny black blip, would reveal any islands in their path, but not manmade objects like a cargo ship that could run over them as easily as a backhoe over sidewalk chalk art.

"Being totally lost in the fog is a terrible thing," Ed says. It removes the option of a good choice vs. a bad choice, and as Skip says, quickly turns you into a believer of providence . . . or fate. "You could react rightly and it ends up the wrong thing to do," Skip says. "You simply live through it or you don't. There is no reason to like fog and nobody, *nobody* does except pilots returning from a bombing run."

Leaving Kjell at the helm, Skipper ("being the light-hearted fellow he is in times of danger," describes Ed) went below and came up with the little air horn—essentially a whipped cream can that makes noise instead of whipped cream and is, in this situation, just about as useful.

"Alright, lads," Skip said. "If we run into trouble, we'll just toot this." And he gave the air horn a little honk.

The minute he did, the elephantine blast of a freighter sounded back at them through the fog. It vibrated in their ears and in the backs of their teeth and on their breastbones for several beats: the sound of a terrifying bassoon, if the bassoon was the size of a walrus. When the blast ended, the only sound was the motor's tiny hum and the licking of the sea against the hull.

Where was the freighter? One hundred yards to starboard? Fifty? Directly off the bow? The sound was too large to pinpoint. "It came from all around us," Kjell remembers. "We thought we were in the middle of the sea lane."

"It was very spectral, spooky," John says. "It sounded like a monster you can only imagine."

They all knew that if the freighter struck them, they could be dead. And the chances of their bodies ever being found were slim to none.

In times of imminent danger, the crew tends to react alike. John went silent, waiting for orders. Ed also clammed up. "I defer to these guys," he explains. "I want to shut up and do as I'm told." Kjell was, in his own terms, "freaking out," but for the sturdy, fjord-raised, thrill-seeking sailor, this translated simply to thinking privately: *I don't really want to be here right this minute.*

As for Skipper, "The weight of responsibility immediately grew heavier on me," he remembers. He elected to turn landward and hug the coastline, putting as much distance between them and the sea lane as possible. The fog stayed just as dense, but the GPS showed that San Juan Island was the closest land mass, and trusting the GPS was better than waiting to be mowed down by invisible water giants.

Then the GPS went out.

Kjell remembers steering slowly in silence, knowing that last he'd seen, the island lay somewhere off their port, but unable to watch the variations in the shoreline. Deep? Shallow? Rocks? Where were they? The GPS stayed black. The fog lowered into a dense, dank blanket. Overhead, blurry tree tops on the island's hillside suddenly appeared, gliding by off the portside like disembodied masts in the white. "We were so close to land," Kjell recalls. "We could almost reach out and touch it. Scared the dickens out of me."

Suddenly Skipper shouted. "Turn to starboard!"

They were heading right for the shoals. Skipper had seen a solitary tree materialize dead ahead. Alone like that, the tree must grow out of an outcropping like a satellite to the island. Shallow water was close. It was here.

Kjell threw the wheel to starboard. The tree melted sharply away. No impact. No scrapes. They had escaped the shallows. Eventually, the fog cleared and the men arrived safely in Victoria, but the day was a strong reminder that at sea, once something goes wrong, danger can pile up fast. And the simplest mishap can quickly metastasize into crisis.

Nevertheless, "I wasn't scared," Skipper remembers, nearly ten years later. ("He never gets scared," Kjell avows.) As always, Skip had a backup plan: Even if they had struck the shoals and sprung a leak, he knew the story of a sailor who once used an apple to plug a hole that was flooding his boat. The apple swelled, the water stopped, and the man sailed like this for three days until he reached land.

"We always have apples," Skip reasons. "And grapefruit! I wonder if a grapefruit would work?"

Kjell rolls his eyes. Heaven forbid the loathsome grapefruit play any useful role on board.

CHAPTER SEVEN

We Are Free

Kjell: In His Own Words

> I wish to have no connection with any ship that does not sail fast; for I intend to go in harm's way.
>
> —JOHN PAUL JONES

My perspective on fifteen years of sailing together is one accompanied by a good dose of humility. How is it that I, having grown up as an agnostic, perhaps even an atheist, can be this privileged to break bread with these Christian men for all these years? Were it not for sailing, perhaps we never would have hung out together; we are of completely different backgrounds and interests. These men have the kind of character I didn't have as a young man—kind, patient, honest—and simply hanging around them for the past decade and a half has taught me how to respond to situations as they arise; to behave more like Christ.

I am known as the King of Norway, but also the daredevil. Here is a story that doesn't explain why this is so, but does prove I have always been this way. My parents, in their infinite wisdom, would let me, at fifteen years old, go out with my sixteen-year-old friend on a little tiny boat for three months with the equivalent of ten dollars in our pockets. And no cell phones, remember. A lot of kids did that in the summer. We would sail down into the fjords where we'd mooch off our buddies who lived further south.

One evening, we were sailing south with the wind on our backs. We fell asleep in the shipping lane of the Oslo fjord . . . and woke up in the open ocean. We were the only living things around as far as the eye could see. No land, no ships, no boats. Nothing but two teenage boys in a sixteen-footer with no outboards, no motors, no food. Just a paddle and the wind. Our sole navigation system was our eyes. We could see the sun and knew we could turn either left or right. We chose left.

Before long, land reappeared. Until now, I had felt no fear. No panic. But when we saw that land on the horizon, I did feel sudden, tremendous relief—the realization, *I could be in the first thirty seconds of death right now.*

All of that is to explain why, today, a little wind or fog with these old guys does not scare me.

I have observed that gradually over the years we go for shorter walks, we eat and drink less, and we go to bed earlier. I think it has something to do with age. The three other guys, you see, are getting older. That is also why comfort trumps everything. We have been discussing the merits of switching to motor yachts rather than sailboats, though the discussion isn't going anywhere. Perhaps when one of us (I suppose that would be me) turns ninety.

Hilaire Belloc once wrote: "The sea drives truth into a man like salt." He is dead right. Relaxing on the water is completely different than relaxing at a pub with a beer and cigar. There are no distractions other than God's creation. Your senses are heightened and you are in the zone of clarity. Your epiphany moments are longer and stronger.

I will always remember the anticipatory feelings we all have when we are in the channel having just left Anacortes: smelling the freshness of the water, putting on another layer of clothing because it is always colder on the boat, checking the gear, figuring out the halyards, waiting for John to announce that lunch will come soon, followed by the first cigar of the voyage.

If I never went sailing again, I would miss feeling and acting younger than our age. Being on the water brings out the youth residing in us with all of its vigor. Life becomes a lot more natural. We are not guarded. We tend to be impulsive and we tell a lot of jokes (well, Ed does for sure). At this stage of our lives we are supposed to be full of wisdom which we dispense left and right. That is all well and good, but for one week in the San Juan Islands every year, life takes another turn and we are free to be ourselves fully.

I am grateful to God for granting me the opportunity to do this with these three friends for fifteen years, soon to be sixteen. We're like the energizer bunny; we keep on trucking.

CHAPTER EIGHT

Deer Harbor

> Ships are the nearest things to dreams
> that hands have ever made.
>
> —ROBERT N. ROSE

HOME OF KILLER HILL

On Orcas Island's west side there hangs a two-fingered peninsula like an upside-down Y. Tucked inside the keyhole-shaped apex of this peninsula is Deer Harbor: a scenic harbor with an island-dotted front yard and a cape of heavily forested slopes flung behind.

The little harbor is both hushed and beautiful. Twelve miles from the ferry landing, the place is in perpetual repose, escaping most of the fishing and whale-watching traffic from the mainland and offering a quiet stop for the sailors, especially after the rococo energy of Victoria. There's no such thing as internet unless you stand perfectly still in a secret spot on the dock that only these sailors know about. Here they can get one bar of connection—just enough to call home and tell their wives that they're alive and on land.

If the men want showers (they do) and don't want to take them on board (they don't), they must reach Deer Harbor before 6:00 PM. Unlike many other harbors, Deer's facilities don't accept quarters, but rather tokens, and these must be purchased at a pint-sized grocery store before the store closes. One token gets you five minutes, which "for this Marine," John says, gesturing to Skip, "is plenty," but is a bit pinched for the King of Norway, who would prefer a larger boat with a more spacious head. And a claw-foot bathtub. And a cabin boy for running errands.

Deer Harbor is also home to one of the men's favorite locations: Killer Hill. After dinner, it's tradition to walk slowly up a particularly steep trail that runs parallel to the shore and carries you up into a world of Douglas firs, giant cedars, and Pacific madrones with their distinctively hued trunks, red like African soil.

"Killer Hill" is not its real name. The epithet was coined by Kjell, still scarred by the memory of the first time they climbed the hill. The men had just consumed an unusually heavy dinner when someone suggested exploring the trail. "Pure and unadulterated pain," Kjell remembers. "I was one step away from a major cardiac event." Listening to all his puffing and wheezing, John told Kjell he should go home and get a personal trainer. Which he did. "Best decision I ever made," Kjell says. Since then, Killer Hill has gotten mysteriously shorter and less steep.

Long or short, the toil is worth it. The top commands a breathtaking view of the sunset over the island-spangled bay. Horizontal light rays bring out different colors in the water, creating an ombré sheet of cobalt that washes out to the palest blue pearl, almost white, on the horizon where it meets distant roaming island shores. On perfect evenings, there is no wind, not a ripple in sight.

The unwritten rule is that few words are spoken. After a few minutes, the men walk back down. The first few years, they made the hike together. This has changed. For various reasons, they now take the walk in pairs or alone. The solitude suits the place. "It is a respite from the busyness of coming into port, tying up, making dinner, banter over dishes," John describes. "A very peaceful time."

BUCKET BRIGADE

For being an almost hypnotically tranquil pit stop, Deer Harbor has attracted its fair share of mishaps and adventures. One year, the men were far north among the smaller islands, navigating south through the archipelago, when Ed stuck his head out of the saloon and called up the ladder: "Is there supposed to be water down here?" One of those rhetorical questions no skipper wishes to hear.

Water was coming in onto the floorboards—a bad sign because all sailboats have a bilge, an empty space below deck that collects incidental water. If water was up to the floorboards, then it had already flooded the bilge.

The first question to settle was whether the boat's freshwater supply had sprung a leak or whether something had holed the boat and they were taking in seawater. "Taste it," Kjell said from the helm. "If it's fresh, it's ours. If it's salty, it's coming in." He was only half joking, but still, nobody tasted it.

Skipper immediately went down into the saloon, pulled the ladder away, and opened the engine compartment. Water had filled the engine well and was approaching the baseline of the engine. Four panels could be opened to reveal the engine itself. These Skipper removed and found nothing. A quick phone call to the boat owner revealed a hidden fifth panel. Skip opened it and there discovered a hose squirting water: the hot water heater.

This gave everyone strong relief. Seawater water could have entered the boat through a leak in any one of hundreds of places. Finding exactly where could have taken hours and by then the water might have swamped and killed the engine and left the men at the mercy of the wind (barely stirring) to navigate to harbor—while still taking in water. Internal flooding, however, was much more manageable because the boat held only sixty to one hundred gallons: not enough to cripple the engine.

While Kjell steered toward Deer Harbor, the others stopped the leak by duct-taping the slit hose, then formed a bucket brigade. Ed used an empty coffee can to scoop water from around the base of the engine and handed it to John, who passed it up the ladder to Skip, who threw it overboard. Scoop by scoop. Kjell motored for as long as he could, then shut off the engine and helped bail while the boat drifted south with the current. After bailing for a while, Kjell flipped the engine back on and motored for a bit, then shut it off and rejoined the brigade.

It was evening by the time they limped into Deer Harbor. Fortunately, insurance covered the damage. Anacortes Yacht Charters arranged for a mechanic to visit the boat and told the men to go to dinner. By the time they returned, said the club, the boat would be fixed.

Dinner was uneventful, and true to the yacht club's word, the boat was ready to relaunch by the time the men returned.

SWAMPING *LEWIS*

Whenever the men sit down to reminisce, there is one subject that receives much discussion, and that is the fact that the question of *who gets to use the lifeboat* has never actually been discussed. The dinghy *Lewis* is marketed as seating four, but, well, the mother ship is also marketed as having a shower (which the men have never used, scorning it in favor of shower stalls on land).

"If we need *Lewis* for lifesaving purposes, we're in trouble," Kjell says. "No way it will hold four large guys." (Most of the men are actually average height and build, but what Kjell means is, "There won't be room for me to take my nap.")

So whom do they sacrifice? The question is broached repeatedly but never decisively answered.

One year, Skipper steered them out of Deer Harbor and around the corner of the peninsula toward Jones Island, a 188-acre bit of land thick with forest and, from the air, shaped rather like an animal cracker's imitation of a prancing sheep with upright ears. About a hundred yards off Jones' rocky shore, Skip anchored the boat and the men prepared to row to shore by twos: one the passenger, one the ferryman making three trips back and forth until all four were on land.

It worked fine in theory.

Lewis has scant freeboard to begin with. As soon as the men sat down, it became negative freeboard. The lifeboat began taking in water while the men rowed as fast as they could to shore. "That's how we got onto the beach," Kjell remembers. "We almost drowned ourselves. So we really need to have this conversation: The day we need to escape in *Lewis*, which guy do we sacrifice?"

"That's the day Kjell ceases to be king," John laughs.

"The easiest question is, *Who's the oldest?*" Skip says. "*Who has lived his life to the fullest?*" Hint: It might be Kjell. It certainly isn't Skip, John, or Ed, though Ed makes a habit of insisting he's ready to leave this earth right now, so perhaps that's his way of volunteering to relinquish his berth on the wee ark. The fact that he has already brushed death's cold shoulder might have something to do with it.

"I've had a heart attack—but I'm not changing my eating habits," he says, scooping up cheese sauce with his chewy Bavarian pretzel. He takes time to shove the French fries closer to Kjell, who is waving his hands again and saying something that rhymes with "no, I shouldn't."

"We're two steps from glory," Ed insists. "Eat the fries!"

At least whoever stays on the mother ship will go down with plenty of food.

THE DAY THE ENGINE DIED

2009 was the year that Paul Kimmell, a mutual friend, joined the crew and they chartered the *Escape*, a German-made boat that was prettier than it was practical. "Not very German at all," complains Ed, the most beleaguered by the boat's little quirks and obnoxious habit of tripping him when he had done nothing at all to offend it. "I don't care about the pretty wood or the nice clocks. Everything was too small. The boat was a head-bumper. I do find the ceiling before anybody else, and I have the propensity to bump my head anyway, but this was stupid. The deck was covered with useless corners. There was stuff to stumble over all over that stupid boat."

The *Escape* did worse than entertain itself tripping Ed. On a hot, windless day, the men were motoring out of Roche eastward toward Deer Harbor when the engine began to clang. The normal sound is a smooth grind; it changed to a knock that grew louder and louder. Just when Skipper decided they should shut it down, the engine died.

Sun. Heat. No breath of wind. The slight forward motion from the current was not enough to provide steerageway, just enough to make the shoals and frequent islands a worry. The *Escape* was already drifting toward one rocky shore. The realization settled across the boat from man to man: *This could be dangerous* simultaneous with *But we got this*.

Skipper radioed Anacortes Yacht Charter, who promised to send help. The men waited on the boat for an hour and a half, floating inch-ways in slow motion beneath the sun. As a last resort, they could always drop anchor to stay in place. But eventually the air stirred just enough for them to hoist the sails and maneuver closer to Deer Harbor. They were still a mile from port when "help" finally arrived in the form of a speck and a high-pitched whine on the horizon.

The men peered into the distance. The whine got louder. The speck grew bigger, but not much. It was a fourteen-foot aluminum dinghy powered by a flustered, underpowered outboard motor and a pair of vice grips where the throttle should be. Steering the boat was a twenty-something girl sitting not on the bench, but on one of those old green-and-white plastic-strap lawn chairs your grandparents threw out in the 1960s because they had already fallen apart. In front of her was a magnificent dumpling, aka her boyfriend. He was in charge of nothing except nearly sinking the boat. A mere inch of freeboard struggled to remain visible: the last man standing in an epic showdown with the boyfriend's gratuitous poundage.

The girl pulled up within safe distance of the *Escape*. "You need a tow?"

The five men could feel the disbelief shifting from one to the next. The *Escape* was thirty-six feet. The dinghy was less than half that and barely staying afloat. Any wave at all would swamp it and its portly cargo in a nanosecond.

"Yes, we need a tow," Skip answered.

"Throw me a line."

He threw her a bow line and she attached it confidently to the dinghy. Skip tied the other end to the tow eye on the bow of the *Escape*. The extraneous boyfriend, meanwhile, hunched industriously on the longsuffering dinghy without contributing anything to the production except a doozy of a plumber's butt. The sailors kept their eyes fixed assiduously elsewhere.

The girl fired up the motor. With the yacht two and half times her size behind her, she began towing them home.

The men were in a bit of shock. Deer Harbor is tricky to enter. Between outcroppings and a small island is only one small passage leading into port. And here they were with no steerageway except what they could manage while being pulled by a twenty-five-foot rope attached to a midget boat with a crummy outboard and a pair of vice grips and two people (one worth three) nearly drowning inside.

The real trick was bringing in the *Escape* with enough speed so that when they detached the rope, Skipper had steerageway, but slow enough that the *Escape* wasn't launched straight into the docks.

Into the marina they came: the dinghy with its caterwauling motor, the *Escape* barging behind. The girl let go the rope and peeled off and Skipper was left steering for the slip on his own. The men realized they were being watched. Sitting on the dock were a couple of spectators, a man and woman, both old and wrinkled and highly curious and fairly naked.

As the *Escape* came in, the senior citizens creaked to their feet, ready to take a line and help haul in the yacht. To their credit (and Skip's relief), they elected instead to help by getting out of the way. John and Ed jumped off the bow and stern like normal and tied off the boat and everything came to a safe and happy end. Except the aged ones were still pretty naked. And the boyfriend still had a plumber's butt. And the men still had a dead boat.

The girl produced a tool kit. As it turned out, she was an electrician too—as multi-talented as her boyfriend was multi-pointless. After a brief inspection, she declared the *Escape*'s engine shot, returned to her dinghy, and zoomed off again into the distance with her mosquito's hum of an engine and her pet bump on a log.

Skipper contacted Anacortes Yacht Charter and everyone agreed on a plan. This was the sailors' second to last day anyway. Leaving the *Escape* in Deer Harbor for the charter club to handle, they would catch a ferry to Anacortes in the morning and be on their way home as scheduled.

If only it were that easy.

Next morning, they called a cab to shuttle them the twelve miles north to Deer Harbor's ferry. Their chariot showed up in the form of a retired highway patrol car with a grand total of five seats: three crammed in the back, one up front, and the fifth consumed by the driver, a vast and cheerful mountain of a woman who could have swallowed the fat boyfriend whole. "That's okay," she said, seeing the men's faces (and their luggage). "We can make two trips."

No, the men said; they couldn't make two trips. No time and no desire to spend twice the money. So they stuffed the trunk with their luggage, and the seats with themselves: five men in four seats, Paul perching on Ed's knees. "Lucky me," Ed recalls with a grimace. John scored the front seat next to their garrulous driver who took off at the speed of sound up the curvy island road wide enough for approximately one and a half cars.

Whiplashing around corners, the driver told them the merry story of her partner in the cab company. The previous night, he had decided he didn't want to drive anymore, so with the cab still in motion, he had opened the door and stepped out. Hilarious, right? Piled on top of each other and clinging to head rests and door handles, all the sailors could do was pray that this crazy lady driver didn't decide to try the same thing.

They arrived disheveled but alive at the ferry dock. Just as the sailors were boarding the ferry, along came a kingly Harley motorcycle saddled by a rider resplendent in leather and a matching Harley helmet. The rider dismounted, put the bike on the kickstand, got ready to walk the bike onto the ferry, pulled off the helmet—and it was the girl who had towed them into Deer Harbor. "This ride sure beats the one you had yesterday!" Ed exclaimed.

The moral of the story is that if that fourteen-foot aluminum dinghy could hold Jabba the Butt and the old patrol car could carry all five of them plus a woman going above and beyond her duty to fill the front seat, then *Lewis* has nothing to worry about. A little freeboard can go a long way. Plus, Ed's lap is always available.

CHAPTER NINE
Roche Harbor

> And the sea will grant each man new hope,
> as sleep brings dreams of home.
>
> —CAPTAIN MARKO RAMIUS,
> *THE HUNT FOR RED OCTOBER* (FILM)

ROCHE HARBOR

Roche Harbor is Kjell's particular favorite. If Friday is charmingly blue-collar, Victoria posh, and Deer rustic, then Roche is something of all three: sheltered yet chic, a popular subject on the easels of local artists, flaunting a slight international flair as a US port of entry. Cupped inside a chink in the northwest tip of San Juan Island and protected by land on all sides, Roche is also significantly warmer than out on the water of the straits. Any jackets the men have been wearing in the bright spring breeze are instantly shed when they enter Roche.

On any given day during the season, as much as several billion dollars' worth of value lies anchored in the harbor. One year, the men were fairly certain that one mega yacht anchored just outside the marina—too large to dock anywhere else—belonged to none other than Oprah.

People-watching in Roche is a favorite sport of the sailors, especially given the throngs of ritzy yacht-dwellers who are there not to see so much as to be seen. Breezily well-attired people parade the docks with their poodles or other dainty breeds that might once have been—hundreds of years ago—remotely related to real dogs.

But most of it is a façade. Roche attracts the wannabe-rich, Kjell explains, more than the actual rich. "I suspect that all of the boat wealth anchored in Roche Harbor is at least ninety percent mortgaged where the boat owners owe their souls to the company store," he says. "They go into deep debt buying their floating edifices, only to be sent into bankruptcy once they encounter difficulties making their payments."

Roche Harbor is also home to, hands down, the men's favorite breakfast place on the planet—the Lime Kiln

Café. They breakfast here at least once every voyage without fail. Given the standard fare of bananas and cereal they consume onboard on other mornings, the men are predisposed to agree that the coffee, eggs, biscuits, potatoes, jam, and especially doughnuts (fried in-house) taste better at the Lime Kiln Café than anywhere else on earth.

When the men aren't eating doughnuts, they might be saving a church from burning down. Sailing into Roche, you can't miss the pristine Chapel of Our Lady of Good Voyage, white as a dove on the forested hillside overlooking the harbor. One year the men decided to have a look. The tiny, century-old chapel greeted them with the silence of a dozen flickering candles. The room was completely empty.

The men were touring the statues of Jesus and Mary, the Lord's table, the paintings on the wall, when one of the candles guttered and fell. Behind it was an event poster on the wall that would have caught flame had not one of the sailors—"It was probably me, because I'm very heroic," Kjell says—rescued the fallen fire.

FOUR GUYS IN A BOAT; WHAT'S THAT ALL ABOUT?

Skipper and the crew might have stared down fog, rocks, and kaput engines, but one late afternoon in Roche they more or less met their match in the form of a bullish female officer from US Customs.

Returning from Victoria, they stopped at the customs dock before re-entering the States. Skipper collected passports and entered the customs shed on the very outskirts of the harbor. The three crew members sat placidly on the boat and awaited his return. They could not have foreseen what he encountered inside and what soon came marching out for inspection.

"A—a woman, " Ed describes delicately. "Very tall and very manly and forthright."

Mid-thirties, easily six-foot-three, well over two hundred pounds, the officer was like "a refrigerator with a head," according to John. She had a gun on her hip and looked like she knew how to use it. And she was pounding toward the boat like she was trying to drive nails into the dock with each step.

To Skipper inside the shed, she had been clearly the senior officer; he could tell the way the male officers shifted away from her when she spoke. "Four guys on a boat—what's that all about?" she had demanded. Her flat voice and sterile eyes had made determining her mood difficult. Skip hadn't been able to tell whether she was asking the question to be conversational or because she suspected them of actually having *fun*. "She might have been testing my response," he says. "A question to rattle me."

Whatever her intent, she had decided to come out and see what "four guys in a boat" was all about. John,

Ed, and Kjell, sitting innocently on the sunny deck like the three wise monkeys, were taken aback at the sight. She was intimidating in the classic way of a needy, insecure bully with something to prove and the perpetual panic that nobody will take their authority seriously. "She was formidable," Ed describes, and he was glad that as an American, surely she was on their side—only she wasn't.

She stared at John, who was halfway through his afternoon's cigar. "Do you have any cigars down below?"

Cigars aren't against regulations, but by her tone, you would think she was asking John if he had smuggled a nuclear warhead, a hundred pounds of cocaine, and a terrorist with a ticking vest below.

"Yes, ma'am," John answered.

"Any of them *Cuban*?"

"No, ma'am."

"Mind if I check?" She wasn't asking.

John led the way down into the cabin where she watched him retrieve all the men's cigars. On deck, she proceeded to scrutinize each one, comparing them with her list of contraband.

"She was like the soup Nazi on *Seinfeld*," Kjell describes. "I tried cracking jokes and she had no sense of humor. Zero."

The officer was staring hard at one of John's. "This is Cuban!"

"No, ma'am, it's Dominican."

"No, it's Cuban."

Skipper stepped in. "It's not a Cuban cigar."

She flourished her paper. "It's on my list."

"Well, they make this brand in Cuba," John explained easily, "but they also make it elsewhere."

"*It's on my list.*"

"Okay," Skipper said, backing off. "It's on your list."

"Here are your choices," she told John. "You can sit here and smoke it right now before you officially enter the country, or you can tear it up and throw it overboard."

The injustice might have gotten under the skin of a scrappier man, but in such situations the even-tempered John is a rule-keeper. The men were hungry; they wanted dinner. Plus, there was the gun. The officer held all the cards—they had zero. Having just finished one cigar, John didn't want to sit on the boat on the US border and spend an hour and a half smoking another, so he took off the wrapper, crumbled up the perfect (non-Cuban) cigar, and threw it overboard.

Lesson learned: Don't smoke cigars when you're checking back into the US.

THE WHALE

"Hitting the rock outside Victoria was in the top two disasters of our experiences," Kjell recalls. "The other was almost getting rammed by a whale."

Whale-watching is a must-do pastime for any visitor aboard anything that floats in the San Juan Islands. The distinctively black and white killer whales, or orcas, the largest members of the dolphin family, populate the chilly Pacific waters where they feed on fish, dolphins, and seals. Anywhere around San Juan Island, the sailors know to keep their eyes peeled for telltale signs of nearby pods.

These signs might be a whale breaching—jumping out of the water—or the famous white spray known as the *blow,* the so-called "water spout" which is a misnomer because orcas do not exhale water; they, like humans, breathe only air. In reality, the white mist spraying in a plume over the ocean is formed by the whale's warm, exhaled breath as it condenses in the cooler, lower-pressure atmosphere, along with any water resting on top of the whale's blowhole. And of course, not so romantically—mucus. (It's a nose, you know.)

A third sign the sailors look for are fast-moving boats that may be no more than pinpricks on the horizon. If the boat holds any bit of orange, they know it's a whale-watching boat with tourists wearing garish survival float suits that make them look like the Stay Puft Marshmallow Man, only orange. And the sailors know that whales are probably close.

Tour boats, with their propellers that could chew up the whales, must park in the water and cross their fingers that the whales swim nearby. Not so with a sailboat. If the men spot traveling whales and the wind is favorable, they turn and sail right alongside the magnificent animals.

"Even at their most boring, they are spectacular," Ed describes. Killer whales often porpoise at the surface: a smooth, energy-efficient, continuous movement where they swim fast enough to soar up and out and back under, over and over, usually at seven or so knots, threading the water with their spindle-shaped bodies. It's a sight that makes you catch your breath, hoping it never ends.

So far, the sailors have seen whales exclusively in a half-moon swath of ocean around San Juan Island: along the southern shore, up the western side of the island through Haro Strait toward Spieden Island and Stuart Island which lie a mile or more distant of San Juan's northern shore.

Nine years in a row, the sailors spotted whales, though the sightings have recently become less frequent. The third or fourth year, they had their most dramatic encounter of all.

Tacking south of San Juan Island one late afternoon, they encountered a pod of a dozen or more whales and began sailing along. Something made the men look behind—and there, a few yards off the starboard quarter, came a massive whale thirty feet long, over half the length of the boat. Swimming right for them. The yacht was six tons. The whale, probably a male at such size, was over six and a half. Colliding at any speed could mean a stove boat, a man (or men) overboard, a full capsize, or even all three at once.

For a brief moment, the crew may or may not have freaked out.

"Okay, guys," said Skipper calmly. "If we need them, the life vests are down there," referring to the storage space beneath the seats.

Just before making contact, the whale dove beneath the boat and disappeared. Seconds later, it resurfaced off the port bow, crested, huffed a lungful through its blowhole and sprayed everyone on board, dove again, and with a mighty leap continued on its merry way. On deck, every pulse was pounding.

"We sorta knew where the life vests were located," Kjell remembers, "but we never wore them." (In fifteen years, the men have regularly worn life vests only since 2015 when John, partly at the insistence of the wives, finally bought thin, unobtrusive vests that would inflate only if you pulled the T-cord or (automatically) if you hit the water. The vests fit like slender harnesses and are so light, the men hardly know they're there.)

Skip analyzes the whale situation as calmly now as he did then. "If we had struck that island in the fog, we wouldn't have died. If we had been hit by the freighter, we probably wouldn't have died." Very matter of fact, like he's estimating how many minutes it takes to get to work. "But the whale . . . I think we could have died."

DALL'S PORPOISES

Perhaps more fun (definitely less dangerous) are the Dall's porpoises, which can be mistaken for dolphins unless you pay attention to their thick, round bellies and small heads which set them apart from the streamlined Flipper. From a distance, the porpoises can also be confused with killer whales thanks to their starkly black and white coloring, like Holstein cows, but at about eight feet long, a porpoise is roughly a third the size of a killer whale. And considerably more playful.

On the first or second year, the men were sailing with a fair wind when a school of about two dozen porpoises decided to join the fun. Swimming furiously off the bow, wheeling around and charging aft, the porpoises treated the yacht like a stage in motion and the sailors their audience. Under sail with such a strong wind, the boat was already flying—and the porpoises kept up, nearly running circles round the boat. The men lay down on the deck and stretched out their hands, all but touching the porpoises as they splashed and pirouetted through the water.

AN ASSASSINATION, AN INTERROGATION, AND THE US COAST GUARD

In 2006, Kjell left the voyage a day early to fly to Thailand for business. The men dropped him off in Friday Harbor and sailed toward Roche, their final stop before returning to Anacortes. Had Kjell known what fun the others were about to have with the US Coast Guard, he probably would have bailed from the plane straight into the Pacific and dogpaddled back to the boat to make a mess of things, with any luck.

Here's how it happened.

Just a week prior, a US airstrike had killed Al Qaeda's leader in Iraq, Abu Musab al-Zarqawi. All America—especially Homeland Security—was on high alert for likely retaliation. Coast Guard vessels patrolling here and there around the islands were always common, especially near harbors, but on this one sunny morning as Skipper, Ed, and John tacked back and forth up the San Juan Channel, a vessel appeared motoring toward them, clearly on a mission.

It was a fast-response cutter, instantly recognizable as Coast Guard by the orange stripe slashing its hull, as well as by the fact that at over one hundred-fifty feet long and armed with a 25-mm autocannon and four .50-caliber machine guns, it looked closer to a small battleship than anything else.

The cutter maintained its approach. On the deck in the aft of the boat, nearly two dozen crew members assembled: sharp-looking guardsmen lining up at ease.

"I wouldn't be surprised if we got boarded," Skipper said.

He tacked starboard toward the cutter. Right on cue, the cutter banked, blocking his exit. The next minute, two orange rigid inflatable boats (RIBs) hit the water from the cutter's rear-launching ramps. With their deep-V hulls, shallow draft, and one or more powerful outboard engines, RIBs are designed for high-speed vessel interception and non-compliant boarding team operations. Basically, kicking butt and taking names on the water. Or on your boat if necessary.

The two RIBs motored with high-stress whines toward the yacht. Each RIB was manned by a driver and four guardsmen in front, two by two. A .50-caliber machine gun sat in the bow. No one manned the machine gun—for now—but the guardsmen didn't have to. Skipper hove to and slowed the yacht.

"No joking," he told John and Ed. "Take this very seriously."

The RIBs pulled off to the yacht's port side about fifty feet away. A voice blared through the bullhorn: "We are the United State Coast Guard. Do you have any firearms or drugs on board?"

"No, we don't!" the men yelled back.

"Prepare to be boarded." The driver of the first RIB zipped over to the yacht in two seconds flat. Off the RIB came four coast guardsmen. As soon as they stepped aboard, the driver zipped away again and stayed off the yacht's port side, presumably to maintain a better angle for the machine gun should he need it. The second RIB remained off the starboard side.

The four guardsmen were young, fit, and professional. Not an inch of fat or nonsense between them. Each bore a sidearm. They also carried a laptop that was quite visibly the worst computer on earth. It looked like the unholy offspring of a briefcase and a metal trash can lid bred at some evil hour of night in your twitchy neighbor's garage in the 1980s. Even Ed, the least techie of the crew, recognized the computer as a piece of junk.

"We're here for a safety inspection," said the senior officer. This was polite (and abbreviated) speak for *Show us the hold so we can determine whether you have a fire extinguisher and life jackets and other safety paraphernalia aboard, which we don't really care about, by the way. You can drown or go down in blazes all you want. We just need to see whether you're harboring guns or drugs or malice for the US.*

Skipper and the officer descended into the hold where the officer proceeded to ply Skipper with questions. Name? Documentation papers? Personal flotation devices? Distress signals? Safe electrical system? Nearly half an hour idled by as the guardsman carefully entered Skip's answers into his ancient mutant mutt of a computer.

Topside, the remaining guardsmen questioned John and Ed. Unlike the virago from customs, the guardsmen were pleasant. Not jovial, but respectful and secure in their authority. John and Ed felt simultaneously very safe—surrounded as they were by firearms, which were presumably in better working condition than the computer—yet tense. They were completely at the Coast Guard's mercy. Imagine being pulled over and questioned by three cops at once and you can't be sure why. No matter how you slice it, they're in control, and you are not.

It wasn't long before John and Ed, listening to the voices in the cabin, realized they were being asked the same questions as Skipper below. They were being tested. Did their answers match up?

Finally the interrogation ended. The senior officer tried to print a copy of the report, as protocol demands, using his trusty little printer about the size of a carton of cigarettes. He pushed *print*. Nothing happened. He pushed it again. Nothing.

And so it happened that the officer became the first person to say a bad word on the boat.

He sent the junior guardsmen back to the mother ship to retrieve NCR paper so he could write the report by hand, which he proceeded to do for the next half hour, asking Skipper the questions all over again. (Why did he not simply read the information off the computer screen?) Finally, the officer turned a copy over to Skip.

Semper paratus, not so semper high-tech.

"Why did you stop us?" Skipper asked. His was one of about ten other boats in the channel. He figured the Coast Guard must have profiled the yacht. *Four guys on a boat,* you know. Very fishy. Definitely at least a Cuban cigar on board.

"You were the closest," came the guardsman's answer. Some profile!

With crisp thanks, the guardsmen took off. So did the second RIB, watching all this time. And the cutter continued on through the channel.

The men hoisted sail and continued on toward Roche Harbor, an hour behind schedule but none the worse off for it. The new adventure already wore a certain glamor.

"It was really neat to watch their protocol," Ed recalls. "And it helped that they were the US Coast Guard—not the Guatemalan! Most of all, it was great to see the skipper once again manage the situation, say what needed to be said, direct us the way we should be. A smart aleck would have caused trouble, but there's no way we were going to do that."

"Good little boys," Skipper agrees.

THE SQUALL

"Sometimes you can see a squall coming," Skipper says. "Sometimes you can't."

That depends on whether the squall comes from across the water, in which case you see it, or whether it drops on you from above, in which case you don't.

Squalls—sudden, dramatic gusts of wind sometimes partnered with rain and lightning—are usually marked by a towering cloud with a flat, blackish base, often shedding visible streaks of dark rain into the ocean. If you can see through or under the cloud, the wind isn't likely to be ferocious. But if the cloud touches the horizon, shape-shifting in hard-edged, oily-looking tufts, you could be in for a savage ride.

Experienced skippers will immediately reef the sails, secure everything below deck, and prepare for a potentially massive windshift. Most squall damage comes from that initial slam of wind. Unleashing with the sound of a thousand screams, the first punch can surprise green sailors with an accidental jibe which sends the boom hurtling across the boat or even snaps the boom in half.

Ships sideways to the wind—the worst possible position—can also suffer a knockdown. Under the wind's ferocious brawl, the boat heels to the point that the bottom of the hull is pried out of the water and the mast lies parallel with the sea. If the boat doesn't recover its balance soon, it might settle into the water, a disastrous position past the point of no return; or the wind and waves could pummel the exposed hull and roll the boat into a full capsize. Upside down, the boat sinks.

This particular squall dropped down on the yacht in the middle of Haro Strait out of a flawless sky. The men were not alone; Kjell had again jumped ship a day early due to work, but replacing him were Brenda Carnahan, Janet Van Nuland, and Jan Sawyer. As the wind picked up speed and foam-tipped waves chopped the sea, Janet and Jan sat in the prow and held onto the rail. Wind in their hair, rain pelting their faces, they watched the day's color erase and the world transform into poisonous black and white except for the seas, heaving in dark, angry green beneath hectic whitecaps. The crew had to shout to be heard as they reefed the sails. The wind tore across the starboard beam at twenty-five knots with gusts so strong that the air was forced back up the sailors' noses as they tried to breathe.

Skipper decided to turn the boat around and head for safe harbor. Roche was closest. Motoring under bare poles, he turned to port. The yacht heaved in a ponderous one-eighty. The wind shrieked. Still clinging to the rails, Jan and Janet began scooting backward toward the relative calm of the cockpit when the yacht pitched with a massive wave and both women slid under the rail. They clung to the safety line for dear life. The boat heeled so mercilessly that Skipper and the crew couldn't leave the cockpit to do anything. Within moments the women managed to pull themselves up and keep scooting.

Just as Janet reached the cockpit, a line snapped free and collided with the enclosure—the Plexiglas shield protecting the cockpit from the worst of wind and rain—and a panel exploded. A shard of plastic flew into the side of Janet's head. For a minute, that's all anyone knew. The hunk had simply disappeared. Janet maintained heroic composure and crawled into the cockpit, where the men discovered her to be miraculously unscathed. The shard had tangled with her hair but left not so much as a scratch.

To the mouth of Roche Harbor, they motored through the storm. Everyone was glad to dock the boat and get out of the weather. Ed, as usual, credits Skipper. "He sailed us out of it. We all hung on and did what we had to do."

TAPS AND THE EAGLE

The crowning moment of each day in the summer in Roche is the colors ceremony. Just before sunset each night, dock staff members lower the flags of Canada, Great Britain, and the United States at the inner harbor. The tradition draws crowds, especially on the Fourth of July. The men have watched the ceremony numerous times over the years, but on the voyage of 2016, John and Skipper witnessed a scene unlike any other.

The ceremony preluded as usual with rousing patriotic music piped from the loudspeakers. Kids ran and shouted, bare feet drumming the wooden docks. Tourists dined on outdoor patios or lounged in gently bobbing boats while the sunset blazed across the harbor. Conversation quieted while the sounds of "O Canada" and "God Save the Queen" floated from the speakers as the Canadian flag was taken down first, followed by Great

Britain. Then it was America's turn. All noise died, and every head turned to Old Glory.

"Ladies and gentlemen," declared a voice through the speakers. "The salute."

A moment of ripped silence. The American flag was still high. The water burned gold except where the troughs of the noiseless ripples held long, traveling crescents of black midnight.

BOOM.

The cannon fired. People holding their breaths or hiking up their shoulders in anticipation jumped, exclaimed, tittered nervously. A second later the echo clattered like shattering rocks across the marina, and a lone bugle sounded Taps. Slowly, the American flag inched down the rope toward hands waiting to catch it, fold it, never let it touch the ground.

Right at that moment, with the trumpet's notes still poised in the air, came soaring overhead a bald eagle. Wings wide. End to end, taller than a tall man. Close enough that you could see the glint of the sun in the glaring yellow iris of each beady eye. A gasp lifted across the crowd, then silence closed again as the eagle glided over the flag, wheeled around in front of the sun, glided back, and disappeared beyond the trees.

Taps ended.

The loudspeakers burst into "The Stars and Stripes Forever" and applause scattered and, as is tradition, the harbor resounded with a cacophony of boat horns honking their own salute, each trying to outdo the other, nearly drowning out John Philip Sousa.

Out of fifteen years of adventures, the story of the bald eagle rivals nearly all the rest. Though Ed and Kjell missed out, the moment has stuck with everyone, yet another reminder for each sailor why they look forward year round to summer when they cram into John's truck, pray for their very lives as they race to Anacortes, stock the boat full of Kjell's favorite foods, and launch from the docks into the channel to catch the wind.

"You just hope you can live long enough to do it another year or two or three, because man, it's getting tough to jump out of that boat!" Ed declares, sipping the last of his beer. "Even for you, John."

"I'll have my back surgery and I'll be ready for June," John vows.

"And I promise to lose weight again," Ed adds. "But seriously, I have gotten so much from these guys that even if I never sailed again, my cup still runs over."

"If you don't make it, we'll send you a postcard," Kjell promises. "If you do, we'll throw you overboard and take pix."

HOMEWARD BOUND . . . OR BACK TO SEA

As often happens, the men tour the San Juans for four days, then the crew returns home while Skipper re-embarks, this time to captain a cruise for his wife and another couple from church, or perhaps just his wife and a number of her lady friends, making it a nearly exclusively female boat.

"That," declares Skip, "is an entirely different book."

"A guy and three girls on a boat," Kjell quips. "What's *that* all about?"

Of all the men, Skipper is the natural choice for returning to sea, and not just because he is the skipper. Ed the romantic, the poet, would sail to England if he could. John has his eye on the South Pacific, while Kjell would love to explore the Greek Islands and, of course, sail again in his beloved fjords where the open ocean is just one accidental nap away. But Skip might be the most taken with sailing for the sake of sailing.

His dreams? To crew on a boat to Hawaii, or from Florida to the Bahamas, or along the coast of Maine, which, besides Alaska, boasts more miles of tidal shoreline than any state. One gets the sense that simply being on the water is enough for Skip. His heart belongs with the next voyage, and the next, and the next, wherever there's wind enough to fill his sails.

CHAPTER TEN

It Was Good

Skipper: In His Own Words

> Now I remembered a captain's honor and his only
> duty: to bring his crew back alive.
> —CARSTEN JENSEN, *WE, THE DROWNED*

For some things, the anticipation is greater than the reality. Not so with sailing. Some people think that four guys in a boat, year after year, must get old. Not so for me.

God uses places as well as people to change a man. Certain things happen in churches, at dinner tables, in hospitals, in classrooms, in foxholes, and yes, in boats that wouldn't happen anywhere else. The boat gives us time to reflect on our lives, sometimes together, sometimes just within ourselves. The same thing could happen with four guys on a ski trip, fly fishing, or back packing, but it couldn't be any better than on the water. Life fades quickly, but the water seems comparatively eternal.

This all helps us think of our mortality, which would be morbid except for Christ. You can go to Texas and as far as you can see, the land is owned by one man. But on the bow of a boat, all you see is owned by the Creator who has made us princes. More now than when we started, we realize that we will one by one disappear from this place at just the right time, in just the right order, and it will make sense in part because we get together every year and reflect on these things.

To make sailing work, you need the right crew. You need people who can become competent but don't need to be in control. Also, being similar in age is helpful, as well as being the same gender. Jan and I have sailed with couples and siblings before and it's fun, but it is not the same.

This is the right crew.

We are not alike; we are very much alike. We grew up differently and in different places. We came to Christ in different ways. But we are all committed to Christ and trust him for ourselves and our families. We also each married up, which is really important. Our kids are important to us. We remember each other's children and celebrate their accomplishments. We have confidence in each other handling the boat not because we believe we won't make a mistake, but because it is okay to be less than perfect. The lads have been forgiving of me and chided me much less than I have them.

I expect, like the last scene in *Chariots of Fire*, we will attend each other's funerals. Worse, we will attend the funerals of each other's wives.

John Krestchmer once said: "The cockpit becomes a confessional; it's difficult to lie at sea." That's an interesting comment, *It is difficult to lie at sea.* But Jonah told the truth on a boat, so I would say Krestchmer is right. Spending so much time with close friends on the water, you play less of a role; you are who you really are. We have an accurate picture of each other. We are less defensive. We kid each other a lot (especially me; I have to guard myself so I don't leave *all* restraint at the dock). No conversation is off limits. With really good Christian friends you can reveal yourself. Such friendship is the closest thing to marriage outside of marriage.

Sailing with the lads has left so many memories for the senses: the sound of the ferry horns, the smells of smoke drifting from a beach campfire, raw diesel, and salty sea. Inside the boat, you get one of the best sounds of all: the lap of water on the hull. This is music telling you you are moving. It says "all is well."

We aren't allowed to sail the chartered yachts after sundown, but Jan and I have taken our own boat out on the water at night. One of the most perfect sailing moments was on our twenty-six-foot Arcadia on Lake Coeur d'Alene, 10:30 on a summer night, under a full moon.

We sailed in a light but sufficient wind for two hours. You could hear all the little night noises from shore; sound carries further across water than land because the water cools the air above it, slowing the soundwaves. Our moorage was near a log boom and you could smell the distinctive, wet aroma of ancient wood, and know you were home from the sea.

On the water, the moon commands your attention. It is all yours. The reflection extends itself directly to you, even as you move along, and it behaves the same to everyone. But that night, except for the moon's reflection, the water was black while the forest was a blizzard of light.

Given the chance, I would prefer to sail on a warm summer's night on waters I know under a full moon, with one or two other people for quiet conversation and reflection . . . and courage, because it is a little spooky.

Sailing has given me some of my best friends, allowing me to be a part of giving something special to the lads. It has given me some of the best moments of my life. I hope that everyone gets a chance to sail at least once in their lives; "everyone" meaning my friends. My enemies can stay home and pout.

I suspect the lads and I will sail together longer than we should because our motto could easily be, *What's the worst thing that could happen? We all die and go to heaven.* We all hope for one more year, and one after that, and then one more.

My hope is that through these stories, my kids realize Jan and I had a good time in life. Our kids are all doing very well, but I can imagine them thinking, *I wish Mom and Dad had more fun.* We did. We do. I hope our kids see that sailing gave us—Jan and me; the lads and me—great enjoyment and involved some of the best relationships you can have. For our grandchildren and great-grandchildren, I want them to see us as real people with real lives, and that it was good.

THE END

Now, bring me that horizon.

www.ingramcontent.com/pod-product-compliance
Lightning Source LLC
Chambersburg PA
CBHW072022110526
44592CB00012B/1403